The Prairie Spirit in
Landscape Gardening

The Prairie Spirit in Landscape Gardening

Wilhelm Miller

Introduction by
Christopher Vernon

University of Massachusetts Press

AMHERST & BOSTON

in association with

Library of American Landscape History

AMHERST

Introduction to this edition © 2002 by Christopher Vernon

This volume is reprinted from the Illinois Agricultural Experiment Station Circular no. 184 published by the Department of Horticulture, College of Agriculture, University of Illinois, Urbana, in November 1915.

Printed in Canada

LC 2001053965
ISBN 1–55849–329–8

Printed and bound by Friesens Corporation

Library of Congress Cataloging-in-Publication Data

Miller, Wilhelm, 1869–1938
     The prairie spirit of landscape gardening / Wilhelm Miller ; introduction by Christopher Vernon.
          p. cm. — (ASLA centennial reprint series)
Originally published: Urbana, Ill. : University of Illinois, 1915.
Includes bibliographical references (p.   ).
     ISBN 1–55849–329–8 (cloth : alk. paper)
1. Prairie gardening. 2. Prairie gardening—Illinois—Chicago Region.
I. Title. II. Centennial reprint series.
     SB434.3 .M56 2002
     635.9'51773—dc21

                                                            2001053965

British Library Cataloguing in Publication data are available.

Contents

Preface

The ASLA Centennial Reprint Series comprises a small library of influential historical books about American landscape architecture. The titles were selected by a committee of distinguished historians and practitioners who identified them as classics, important in shaping design, planting, planning, and stewardship practices in the field and still relevant today. Each is reprinted from the original edition and introduced by a new essay that provides historical and contemporary perspective. The project was undertaken by the Library of American Landscape History to commemorate the 1999 centennial of the American Society of Landscape Architects. The series is funded by the Viburnum Foundation, Rochester, New York.

The Prairie Spirit of Landscape Gardening has long been considered one of the profession's landmark texts, yet its purposes and inspiration have been enigmatic. The slim, richly illustrated circular was published in 1915 by the Illinois Agricultural Experiment Station and distributed free to anyone in the state who signed a promise to do some "permanent ornamental planting." Wilhelm Miller's text promoted the idea that fine landscape design depended on the use of regional plants and on naturally occurring landforms, especially the horizontal and "democratic" lines of the prairie, which, by Miller's day, was almost entirely consumed by suburban development and agriculture. Miller's recommendations stemmed from a desire, he wrote, to "keep alive the hope of freedom, prosperity, and a life amid more beautiful surroundings."

Throughout his text Miller contrasted his presentation of the prairie style with an "effeminate" East Coast tendency toward formality and a lingering taste for the gardenesque. He was emphatic in his disapproval of tender bedding plants, showy foliage ("variegated rubbish"), and spectacular forms, such as Norway spruce—"rip saws" of the skyline. Miller's horticultural recommendations were aimed primarily at homeowners, but he also intended to influence the design of midwestern farms, parks, and cemeteries.

Christopher Vernon's new introduction casts welcome light on Miller's motives in writing the circular and on the charged moment that occasioned its publication. Miller's prairie style recommendations were grounded in the broad-based imperative to encourage country life, such as that inspiring the magazine *Country Life in America*, of which Miller was an editor. The country life movement arose in counterpoint to the accelerating transformation from rural to suburban and urban life then occurring in the United States. Miller's aim—to make rural communities "so comfortable and beautiful that her children will always wish to live [there] and share in the perfecting of our civilization"—reflected the Reform Era notion that the agrarian past of the United States held the key to its civilized future.

Vernon's introduction also presents an engaging biographical sketch of Wilhelm Miller (1869–1938), about whom little has been written. He chronicles the horticulturist's childhood in Detroit, Michigan, Miller's undergraduate education at the University of Michigan, his master's and doctoral work at Cornell University, his post as horticultural editor of *Country Life in America* under Liberty Hyde Bailey, and his emergence as a major stylistic voice in the boom years of the American Country Place Era. Vernon's essay examines the genesis of the Prairie School, which he traces to the architect Frank Lloyd Wright, and the Chicago School. He discusses the landscape architectural manifestations of the movement in the works of Jens Jensen, O. C. Simonds, Walter Burley Griffin, and others, some of whom were, in fact, hesitant about the affiliation because they conducted national practices.

Jens Jensen (1860–1951) was most sympathetic to the purity of Miller's approach, and his work is heavily represented in Miller's text. Evocative period photographs of the fantastic primeval landscape he designed for the glass conservatory at Garfield Park, the prairie rivers of Humboldt Park, and several private estates demonstrate Jensen working at the top of his form. The work of O. C. Simonds (1855–1932) is also shown in several photographs in Miller's circular, particularly Chicago's Graceland Cemetery, which, Miller noted, exerted a strong influence on home gardeners in the Midwest and elsewhere.

Students of American landscape history will find Miller's text a significant early example of ecological writing—it was strongly influenced by Henry C. Cowles, author of *The Plant Societies of Chicago and Vicinity*—and the historic expression of an emerging conservation ethic. Miller was one of the first writers of national note to urge readers to plant wisely, save trees, protect watercourses, and preserve historic buildings—themes that are repeated throughout his text. The urgent tone of *The Prairie Spirit* testifies to the drama of a watershed moment in American landscape history and the conflict of cultural values defining it. Miller's text is arguably the first that identified an American sense of place, which was made suddenly, ironically distinctive because it was endangered. Miller's book provides a poignant glimpse down a country road, not taken.

To further vitalize the connections between Miller's book and current environmental and design concerns, LALH has invited The Morton Arboretum in Lisle, Illinois, to join us as an educational partner in celebrating the appearance of the reprint. We are pleased to be working with them to bring the timely perspectives of Wilhelm Miller to a wider audience.

Robin Karson, Executive Director
Library of American Landscape History
Amherst, Massachusetts

Library of American Landscape History, Inc., a nonprofit organization, produces books and exhibitions about American landscape history. Its mission is to educate and thereby promote thoughtful stewardship of the land.

LIBRARY of

AMERICAN
LANDSCAPE
HISTORY

Introduction to the Reprint Edition

CHRISTOPHER VERNON

> . . . to the land vaguely realizing westward
> But still unstoried, artless, unenhanced,
> Such as she was, such as she would become.
> Robert Frost, "The Gift Outright"

"Prairie Spirit." "Prairie School." "Prairie Style." These terms were coined by horticulturalist, author, and academic Wilhelm Tyler Miller (1869–1938) (fig. 1). Although Miller's terminology was primarily conceived in reference to landscape design, today it often evokes the more popular architectural imagery of Frank Lloyd Wright's (1867–1959) "prairie houses." In 1958, having consulted the legendary architect, Grant Carpenter Manson concluded that the low, earthbound forms of Wright's houses were inspired by their namesake, the prairies of the American Middle West. He wrote that "the most convincing evidence that Wright and his pupils . . . constantly had in mind the ecology of the region . . . is afforded by the close cooperation which they sought with certain Chicago landscape gardeners who were spreading the doctrine of letting the modest beauty of the prairie speak for itself: Jens Jensen, Walter Burley Griffin, Wilhelm Miller and others."[1] Manson, in support of his claim, cites a source seemingly removed from the literature of architecture, a 1915 University of Illinois Agricultural Experiment Station circular, *The Prairie Spirit in Landscape Gardening*, by Wilhelm Miller.

Miller's treatise, apart from its limited discussion of Wright's architecture, more importantly gave the landscape designs of Jens Jensen (1860–1951) and—to a lesser extent—Ossian Cole Simonds (1851–1931) their first marked recognition.[2] Miller also highlighted architect Griffin's (1876–1937) lesser-known abilities as a landscape architect. This is significant as Griffin was then (and is now) known more as Wright's architect pupil. Despite these important historical observations, Miller's circular proved ephemeral and was largely forgotten by the time of his death in 1938. Manson rediscovered *The Prairie Spirit* for a new generation of readers.[3]

Today, Wilhelm Miller is still principally remembered as the author of *The Prairie Spirit in Landscape Gardening*, though his publications numbered in the hundreds (see Bibliography). The subsequent categorization of Miller as primarily a regionalist has been at least partly due to his frequent use of the adjective "prairie." Indeed regionalism, as qualified by the prairie spirit, was important to Miller, though it represented but one component of his larger landscape vision. For him, regionalism was a means with which to move into a more nationalized future. In his vision, future American gardens would have their design genesis in the evocation and conservation of the primeval—the native landscape that existed "when the first white man came."[4] The temporal dimension is important: in Miller's day (as still in our own), such landscapes were disappearing and, in Jensen's words, of "vanishing beauty" (1).

This introduction seeks to enrich understanding of Miller's theoretical enterprise by—as he did—crossing the boundaries of professional disciplines. Consequently, it draws upon relevant literature both from architecture and from landscape architecture. The essay first explores the evolution of Wilhelm Miller's interest in gardens, a passion that culminated with his literary construction of the "Prairie School." It then examines Jens Jensen's catalytic role in the maturation and codification of the "prairie style" and suggests that Wright and his contemporaries' architecture played a vital role in forming Jensen's and Miller's thinking. Also surveyed are Miller's little-known endeavors as a landscape architect, following *The Prairie Spirit* and his exit from academia. The essay proposes that the publication of *The Prairie Spirit in Landscape Gardening* marked the culmination of Miller's fifteen-year quest to define a national American landscape design aesthetic.

The youngest of four children, Wilhelm Tyler Miller was born on 14 November 1869 at Duane, Virginia, and grew up in Detroit, Michigan, at the edge of the prairie hinterlands.[5] Miller's father, Albert, was a musician and teacher, educated at the University of Jena in Germany. After emigrating to the United States, Albert Miller came into contact with noted literary historian Moses Coit Tyler (1835–1900) at the Ypsilanti, Michigan, Normal School, and in 1856 married Tyler's sister, Olive.[6] Much of Wilhelm's childhood was spent around his father's "big, square piano" listening to the "music of the masters."[7] In keeping with family tradition, Wilhelm Miller enrolled at the University of Michigan and was graduated with a Bachelor of Arts degree in 1892. By this time he had developed an "avid hunger to know the world of plant life."[8] Consequently, Moses Tyler suggested that Miller "harness his sentimental interest in nature by studying horticulture under Liberty Hyde Bailey."[9] Bailey (1858–1954), a Michigan native then at Cornell University, already was celebrated as a botanist and agriculturalist and increasingly for his progressive social concerns. Miller began graduate studies at Cornell in 1895, and under Bailey's supervision he received master's (1897) and doctoral (1900) degrees in horticulture. Both of his dissertations comprised studies of individual flowers, the chrysanthemum and dalhia. Given Miller's specific interest then in the single plant, and the fact that he was later to become known for his ideas on the broadest of landscape designs, it is important to know when his interest broadened and shifted focus.

One of Miller's earliest articles appeared in *Garden and Forest: A Journal of Horticulture, Landscape Art, and Forestry* in 1895, the year he entered Cornell.[10] The subject—test results of new chrysanthemum varieties—is less important than the fact that it was published here, rather than in a scientific journal devoted more exclusively to floriculture. *Garden and Forest* was effectively a surrogate journal for the emerging profession of landscape architecture. That Miller continued to publish articles in the journal suggests his comprehensive knowledge of and empathy with its contents; *Garden and Forest* was one of the earliest sources for his increasing awareness of landscape design. Here, for instance, Miller undoubtedly gained a familiarity with the work of America's premier landscape architect, Frederick Law Olmsted (1822–1903).[11]

Figure 1. Wilhelm Tyler Miller. From *Country Life in America*, December 1912.

We know that Miller's interest in gardens had grown markedly by 1897, when he began employment with Bailey at Cornell's Agricultural Experiment Station. That year, in a station circular, Miller interjected into his text, otherwise devoted to evaluating dahlia varieties, the following: "The place for dahlias is the garden. . . . I believe in flowerbeds, but not in the middle of a beautiful green lawn. The grass has a quiet story to tell, and if dahlias intrude they should be put out for disturbing the peace. . . . I enjoy especially those gardens that have one theme, one central feature, no matter what are the modifications."[12] This passage testifies to Miller's nascent interest in gardens and reveals his early stylistic preference for the open lawn, framed by trees and shrubs. Flower beds were best integrated into the entire composition rather than indiscriminately "scattered." Such "gardenesque" planting beds had been an indulgence of Victorian eclecticism (fig. 2).

In 1898 Miller was hired as a writer and associate editor for Bailey's classic *Cyclopedia of American Horticulture* of 1900.[13] One of Miller's first editorial tasks was to survey the whole of American landscape gardening. He consequently attended "illustrated lectures" and "handled nearly every important book" on landscape gardening.[14] That the scope of Miller's interest had continued to broaden is evinced in his reply to a query concerning the *Cyclopedia's* essay on the landscape cemetery. In this 1898 letter Miller declared that he was "thoroughly in sympathy with the natural or English school of landscape gardening, of which [A. J.] Downing [1815–1852] and Olmsted were the great exponents in America."[15] Foreshadowing the regional orientation of his later work, Miller also acknowledged familiarity with O. C. Simonds's design of Chicago's Graceland Cemetery. According to Miller, Simonds had used "the most advanced ideas of landscape and cemetery gardening" to transform "the raw prairie" into "one of the loveliest places imaginable."

Also important is Miller's essay on Downing, written between 1898 and 1899 for the *Cyclopedia*.[16] Miller concluded that it "would be difficult to overestimate the influence of Downing. He created American landscape gardening." Miller's regard stemmed from his belief that Downing was the "first great practitioner" of the "English or natural school of landscape gardening in distinction from all artificial schools, as the Italian and the Dutch." Miller was now to adopt Downing's role as a popularizer, if not arbiter, of landscape

taste. He would not fail to make mention of Downing fifteen years later in *The Prairie Spirit*.

Miller's Cornell experiences set the trajectory for the remainder of his career. By 1900, the year he received his doctorate, he had embarked upon a literary pursuit of his principles, preparing several publications for popular, rural audiences.[17] Miller's interests were fostered by his mentor, Bailey. Bailey's own garden interests, however, were but one prescriptive dimension of his belief that it was "the lack of cheer in color and interest about the home which is largely responsible for the dissatisfaction of young people with the country," versus the attraction of the city.[18] This burgeoning concern reflected the larger Progressive reform ethos which underpinned Bailey's social vision; Bailey later served on President Theodore Roosevelt's Country Life Commission and investigated various means by which country life might be improved. Miller's most profound debt to Bailey was his adoption of his mentor's Progressive ideals as a sociopolitical platform or motivation for landscape gardening.

Miller's association with Bailey and his publishing projects continued after he left Cornell. In 1901 he became the horticultural editor of the newly created *Country Life in America* magazine—most likely at general editor Bailey's request. The appearance of *Country Life* signaled a growing American interest in country life engendered by the accelerating pace of urban development. Central to its lure was the potential for expansive gardens. In noting the launch of the New York–based magazine, the editors of *The Architectural Record* recognized its garden content and noted that

THE GAUDY WAY OF PLANTING A LAWN

Which intoxicates beginners the world over. The plants are scattered, so as to make the biggest show. Ninety per cent are foreign or artificial varieties, e.g., cut-leaved, weeping, and variegated shrubs, or tender foliage plants and double flowers, such as cannas, .

Figure 2. "The Gaudy Way of Planting a Lawn." Reproduction of Miller's lantern slide. *Author's collection.*

"a hot fight is on between the advocates of the formal and the so-called 'natural' garden."[19] Wilhelm Miller, through his writing and editing for *Country Life*, not only joined in the fight as an ally of the natural garden but soon would expand the battlefront to include the establishment of a specifically American garden.

In 1903 evidence that Miller's ideas on gardens had coalesced appeared twice in print. First of these indications was a brief book chapter, "Scattered Planting vs. Masses."[20] Here he made explicit the form implications of his garden ideals, urging that one should frame and define a lawn with masses of native trees and shrubs, composed in a "nature-like" manner. This outlook contrasted with scattered planting, which Miller believed did not result in a large enough total "picture." He emphasized that masses of hardy native vegetation demanded much less care than "rare and costly plants." Miller's rationale suggests a familiarity with William Robinson's (1838–1935) similar arguments for the British "wild garden." Although his approach would gain further dimension, Miller's essential advocacy of using native plants in a pictorial, nature-like manner was now firmly in place and became the foundation of his effort to establish native American, and later, Prairie School ideals. His promotion of native plants owing to their inexpensiveness and hardiness became a hallmark of Miller's writings.

Also in 1903 Miller published "An American Idea in Landscape Art" in *Country Life in America*.[21] He again advocated the "pictorial" as a means of composition and singled out the landscaped cemetery as an especially noteworthy American phenomenon. Repeating sentiments privately expressed five years earlier, Miller again praised O. C. Simonds's Graceland Cemetery. Landscape and garden design—as differentiated from botany or horticulture—were now the more generalized foci of Miller's attention. Miller's discussion of Graceland marked the first time that he publicly lauded a middle western design example—in a magazine otherwise directed to an eastern audience—and, furthermore, designated it as "American." Ultimately Miller would identify nature-like compositions of hardy native plants with a more telling and convincing Americanism. Moreover, for Miller, Graceland would prove to be a lodestone for design innovation and, over a decade later, the landscaped cemetery figured prominently in *The Prairie Spirit*.

By 1908 Miller's interest in achieving an American style of gardening pervaded his writings. A study trip to England that year introduced him to William Robinson, and he visited Robinson's celebrated home and garden, Gravetye Manor. Miller published the results of his study in a book, *What England Can Teach Us about Gardening*.[22] Therein he postulated that the key to creating an American garden style was the readaptation of English naturalistic planting techniques through the use of largely native plants. Although his conclusions were still to a degree tenuous, for him the use of native plants had become inextricably linked to the notion of an American style. Miller's travels in England appeared to reinforce views already in place. But it was to be rather Jens Jensen and the American Middle West, not Robinson and England, that provided the more profound stimulus.

Wilhelm Miller journeyed to Chicago in 1911 where he met Jensen and saw his work.[23] The two found themselves to be kindred spirits and began a friendship that continued until Miller's death in 1938. In September 1911 Miller introduced his largely eastern *Country Life* readership to a new, Chicago-based landscape phenomenon, reporting that "the great landscape artists of the Middle West love the prairie and use its horizontal lines in their art."[24] In Jensen's work, Miller discovered that his national agenda could be

given local expression. From this date Miller's writings reflected a middle western regionalism; his nationalist motivation receded, though it was never abandoned.

After nearly a decade of writing and editing for *Country Life*—and since 1905 for *The Garden Magazine*—and lured by the opportunity to "practice what he preached," Miller accepted a faculty position at the University of Illinois in 1912.[25] Also influential in Miller's decision to relocate was that *Country Life* had become almost entirely oriented toward satisfying the decorative and status-driven whims of an audience of eastern sophisticates. This shift—an effective abandonment of the magazine's Progressive ideals—already had led Bailey to resign as its editor in 1903. In contrast to the magazine's focus, Miller's Illinois work—not inconsistent with his earlier Cornell activities—would have a more rural and agricultural articulation and engagement.[26] "If Boston is not a geographical entity but a state of mind," Miller wrote from Illinois, "then the Middle West is a state of soul and its spirit is progressiveness."[27] Miller now believed that an American style could first be realized in a region that seemed to be less burdened by European tradition.

The Illinois to which Miller came in 1912 was not, however, without immediate nativist design precedent. Chicago was already perceived nationally as the epicenter of a new architectural movement. As early as the 1890s, works by the architect Louis Sullivan (1856–1924)—such as his celebrated Transportation Building at Chicago's 1893 World's Columbian Exposition—and by his protégé Frank Lloyd Wright signaled dramatic departure from convention, if not revolution. Local architect and critic Thomas Tallmadge (1876–1940) labeled the movement the "Chicago School" in 1908.[28] And Jensen by then had laid the foundations for what Miller would term the "Prairie School of Landscape Gardening." Underscoring Jensen's significance for Miller is the fact that prior to their first meeting neither regionalism nor the prairie was given any prominence in Miller's writings. In the evolution of the Chicago or Prairie School, Wilhelm Miller was a late arrival. Given this sequence, it is vital to examine the local milieu in which Miller so quickly immersed himself. This can be best understood through an examination of the prairie ideal, already present in Jensen's designs, especially as it informed Miller's conceptualization of the prairie style.

Shortly after Jensen was hired by Chicago's West Parks District in 1886, he began to experiment with designs that included a composite of native plants and exotic varieties. Observing that the latter types did not thrive as well in the Chicago soil, he turned toward the exclusive use of natives. Not only were the native plants hardier; they were inexpensively obtained by transplantation from the nearby woods and fields. Successful in cultivating native plants, Jensen in about 1888 created an "American garden" composed almost exclusively of native shrubs and wildflowers in Chicago's Union Park (fig. 3).[29] Jensen's nationalistic label reflected the garden's contents, however, not its style. In design, as depicted in the one surviving plan, this American garden of Jensen's reflected Miller's 1897 ideal of an open lawn, framed and defined by masses of native vegetation.

In 1900, at age forty, Jensen was fired from the park district (owing to his refusal to participate in the political graft pervading the organization) and launched a private practice. The self-taught landscape architect had previously designed in both the formal and natural styles; by 1900, however, evidence of Jensen's growing stylistic preference for the natural, at least within the context of flower gardens, appeared in print. Writing in Chicago's *Park and*

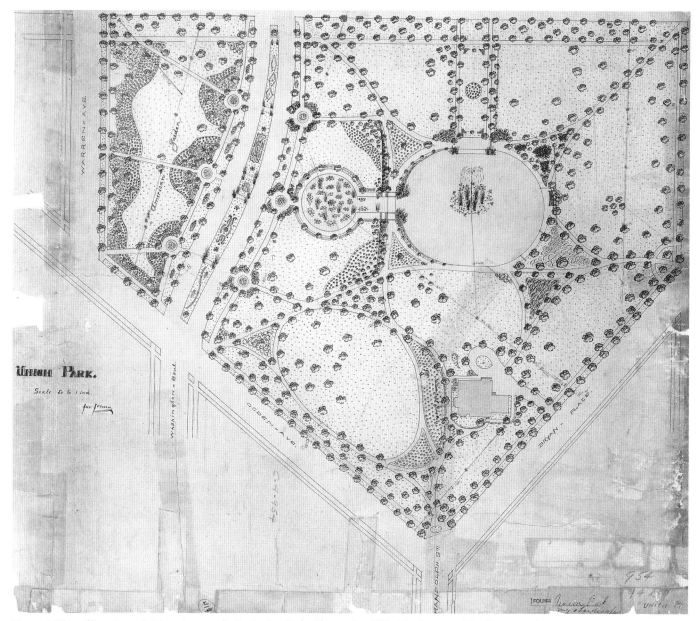

Figure 3. Plan of Jens Jensen's "American garden" at Union Park, Chicago (ca. 1888–94). *Courtesy of the Chicago Park District.*

Cemetery magazine, Jensen explained that the "natural garden" was "the very opposite of the garden of symmetrical design."[30] Although he did not explicitly reveal why, Jensen believed that the natural garden, "fitting in place everywhere," was "the garden for the poor and rich alike." These were preliminary clues to his destination, and several more years of experimentation would pass until Jensen could finally link his landscape designs to the larger indigenous Illinois landscape.

Early textual evidence for when Jensen made this connection appears in 1906, when he published an essay entitled "Landscape Art—An Inspiration from the Western Plains."[31] Here, perhaps for the first time, Jensen explained that it was from "this grand landscape" that he drew his inspiration. Redirecting the national orientation of the "American garden," Jensen was increasingly preoccupied with the Chicago region. He illustrated the article with views of his recently completed work at the suburban Chicago home of Harry Rubens, begun in 1903. One picture especially is

pertinent to Jensen's words: a photograph depicting a lagoon of his own creation. The Rubens lagoon became a design feature—"prairie rivers," as he later named them—which came to be one of his hallmarks. The photograph was captioned only "Simple, Charming, and Lovely" and is without textual reference, but indicative of the aqueous feature's significance is the inclusion of two views of the Rubens prairie river in Miller's *The Prairie Spirit* nearly a decade later; here the captions reveal that Jensen's "aim was to re-create an Illinois water system in miniature; spring, brook, cascade, river, and lake" (13). Miller also mentioned, with the designer as his source, that the Rubens lagoon was the "first attempt to epitomize the beauty of Illinois rivers" (3).[32] The Rubens estate was the site of another design first for Jensen as well. It was here, Jensen recollected, that he first employed "the stratified rock underlying our great prairie country."[33] Such geological formations are to be found along watercourse margins and inland as upheavals, and Jensen's striated prairie rockwork, along with his prairie rivers, became a second distinguishing feature of his work. As with the prairie river, however, discussion of the striated rockwork was not included in his 1906 text, nor was it featured in the accompanying illustrations. That Jensen viewed the rock and water features not as definitive statements but as experiments perhaps explains these omissions. Jensen described the Rubens open lawn as a "meadow" (a more Olmstedian term), not a plain or even a prairie. Nonetheless, the Rubens design confirms that by 1906 Jensen had already identified the larger native landscape as his source of design inspiration.

The architect of the Rubens house also merits consideration. George W. Maher (1864–1926), a Sullivan protégé and member of the Chicago School, was Jensen's sympathetic collaborator in this and other commissions. In his own 1906 essay "The Western Spirit" Maher mused: "Must it be said that the nature which surrounds us is unworthy of art expression? That the men and women we meet must admire the Greek leafage and flora [of classicism] and not the flower of our fields? Does nature around us ape that of the Greek or Goth? Is not our landscape beautiful, grand beyond expression?"[34] Given their similar sentiment for the local landscape, architect and landscape architect likely had influence on each other's thinking.

Several indications of the further evolution of Jensen's design approach appear in 1908. Enlarging upon the regional inspiration encapsulated in the Rubens design, Jensen identified another peculiarity of the prairies. In a 1908 article he explained to a national audience that "here on the western plains we admire horizontal lines so much; lines that are characteristic of the plains themselves."[35] And a photograph illustrating another Jensen article confirms that, also by 1908, he had applied his striated rockwork and prairie river techniques again, this time at Chicago's Humboldt Park.[36] Also around 1908 Jensen acquired property in suburban Ravinia, Illinois, where, in developing his own garden, the first of his characteristic "council rings" (a circular bench constructed of local stone) appeared.

Throughout this period, the West Chicago Parks—as Graceland had for Simonds—served as proving grounds for Jensen's design experiments. By 1910 the work here was distinctive enough to capture the attention of Frank Waugh (1869–1943), a landscape architect, writer, and educator at the Massachusetts Agricultural College (now the University of Massachusetts Amherst). In that year, Waugh promoted Jensen in his book *The Landscape Beautiful*.[37] For Waugh, Jensen's work was "original, novel, [and broke] clear away from the formulas now familiar in America."[38] Waugh found it difficult, however, to isolate and describe the attributes of the work's originality and novelty. He consulted with the designer and reported that "Jensen himself says that he has received his chief inspiration from the Zuni Indians and from the flat, level prairies."[39] Apart from its enigmatic reference to an Amerindian tribe of the southwestern United States, this passage is perhaps the first instance in which Jensen used the term "prairie"—not "meadow" or "plains"—to identify his source of inspiration. *The Landscape Beautiful* was aimed at a national, popular audience. Waugh's praise likely was the most prominent identification Jensen—then known only regionally—had received to date, and it was this book which might have first alerted Miller to Jensen's work.[40]

By the close of the first decade of the new century, most if not all of the key concepts and features of Jensen's mature style were in place, though evolution and refinement continued. By 1912 Jensen had further refined his native planting technique. That year he delivered a lecture—"Let Nature Be Your Teacher"—to the membership of the Illinois Chapter of the American Institute of Architects (AIA).[41] Onto a general archetype of the idealized imagery of

the picturesque, Jensen grafted a more specific model—the plains.[42] This more localized nature, Jensen explained to his audience, included "treasures," which were "as ideal and as beautiful as anything else in the world, including the vegetation and stratified rock." Furthermore, he said, "vegetation should be harmonious; certain trees are for the low lands and certain trees belong to the highlands." This dictim stemmed from Jensen's botanical excursions and suggests his familiarity with the ecological concept of plant associations. As early as 1904, Jensen, an avid naturalist, had published his field studies of the relations among vegetation, soil, and landform, though these were more botanical studies than design polemics.[43] Now, eight years later, he associated particular plants with particular landform and soil configurations within the context of landscape design, instructing that such associations were imitable in design.

Yet to limit our search to the evolution of Jensen's design approach to landscape gardening—or to imagine him as a solitary "prophet in the wilderness"—would deprive us of additional knowledge of the richness of Chicago's contemporary architectural scene. The coalescence of Jensen's "prairie style" coincides with the move of his private practice to Chicago's Steinway Hall in 1908—the year Tallmadge codified the "Chicago School" in architecture. The building was designed by Dwight Perkins (1867–1941), with whom Jensen had earlier served on Chicago's Special Park Commission. Most important, Steinway Hall was a haven for the progressive architects of the day. When Jensen opened his office, Irving (1857–1937) and Allen (1858–1929) Pond, Robert C. Spencer Jr. (1865–1953), and Walter Burley Griffin maintained studios in the building, and Louis Sullivan was a recurrent visitor.[44] It was in this environment that Jensen's tentative experiments no doubt gained resolution and reinforcement. Steinway Hall would remain the locus of Jensen's practice until 1918. Along with these communal offices, Jensen also maintained memberships in several Chicago professional and civic organizations in common with these architects. Beginning in 1905, for instance, he shared membership in the Chicago Architectural Club with Spencer and Griffin, among others. Jensen displayed his work in the club's annual exhibitions on at least two occasions.[45] Jensen's lectures for colleagues—such as "Let Nature Be Your Teacher"—confirm the fluidity of professional boundaries and suggest an ease of lateral movement. Thus there were explicit opportunities for the cross-fertilization of ideas. Griffin, Spencer, and Maher, for instance, were in Jensen's AIA lecture audience (Miller would later link the three as proponents of the Prairie School). And Jensen designed, sometimes collaboratively, garden settings for buildings designed by many of these architects, including Tallmadge, Spencer, Maher, Sullivan, and Wright.[46] These circumstances collectively suggest that Jensen adopted the ideal of the prairie as design inspiration from the architects.

As early as the 1890s, when Jensen's practice of landscape architecture was still nascent, Frank Lloyd Wright drew architectural inspiration from and made explicit reference to the larger prairie landscape.[47] In his 1895 design of the Chauncey Williams residence at River Forest, Illinois, he incorporated boulders—collected by Wright and his clients from the nearby Des Plaines River—into the exterior fabric of the house, massing them at its foundation and framing the entry (fig. 4). The boulders served two important purposes. First, through their strategic placement, they visually anchored the house to its level site. Second and most significantly, the boulders evoked the glacial origins of the landscape. This symbolism, said Grant Manson, "furnishes an insight into the youthful enthusiasm of these people for a new, indigenous architecture growing from the native landscape and expressing its

Figure 4. Chauncey Williams residence (1895) at River Forest, Illinois. Frank Lloyd Wright, architect. Photo by William Gray Purcell. *Courtesy of the Northwest Architectural Archives.*

innermost meaning."[48] Five years later, these affinities between Wright's work and its larger landscape setting received notice in the professional press. In 1900 his friend and fellow Chicago architect Robert Spencer characterized Wright as "a younger man who has scorned [the] easy and popular route"—the use of imitative, historical styles of overseas origin.[49] Instead, Spencer explained, Wright drew local inspiration, "swinging easily along amid the beauties of the forests and flower-sown prairies of his own country."[50] In its reference to nature in its actuality, Spencer's text is pervaded with vegetal metaphor. "If we are to have a real basis for a great national architecture," he asserted, then "our beautiful buildings must not be the forced fruits of an artificial civilization, but must be the natural bloom of a hardy native growth with its roots deep in the soil."[51] Not unlike the way in which Miller and Jensen would identify indigenous nature as the point-of-beginning for an American garden archetype, Wright and Spencer (and Sullivan) saw the natural world as the germinal source for an American architecture. Published in *Architectural Review*, Spencer's essay was one of the first to comprehensively explain Wright's architecture to a national audience. It is not unlikely that Miller read the essay; it certainly would not have gone unnoticed by Jensen. In fact, Jensen later collaborated more than once with Spencer and shared a Steinway Hall tenancy with him.[52]

By 1900 Wright had developed a marked interest in landscape architecture per se, delivering a lecture on the subject that year.[53] In 1901 he employed the architect and landscape architect Griffin, who studied, in parallel with architecture, landscape gardening and horticulture at the University of Illinois. The same year,

Wright made explicit the connection between his architecture and the regional landscape in the pages of the *Ladies' Home Journal*. He explained to a national audience that the form of his "Home in a Prairie Town" prototype "recognizes the influence of the prairie, is firmly and broadly associated with the site, and makes a feature of its quiet level. The low terraces and broad eaves are designed to accentuate the quiet level and complete the harmonious relationship."[54] Later, in assessing his own work up to 1908, Wright similarly urged his colleagues to appreciate that "the prairie has a beauty of its own and we should recognize and accentuate this natural beauty, its quiet level."[55] "Hence," Wright explained, his houses were distinguished by their "gently sloping roofs, low proportions, quiet sky lines, suppressed heavy-set chimneys and sheltering overhangs, low terraces and out-reaching walls sequestering private gardens" (fig. 5).[56] Arguably, Jens Jensen, also Wright's close friend and collaborator, first adopted the prairie metaphor from Wright (fig. 6). Although the prairie's significance for the architect was abstract and metaphorical, it offered the landscape architect not only a potent metaphor but also a literal design model.

In October 1912 Wilhelm Miller, along with his wife, Mary Farrand Rogers (1868–1971), and their two children, moved from New York to Urbana.[57] Miller was at the height of his popularity and known nationally as a horticultural and garden authority. His repute stemmed from his numerous publications, which were distinguished by his accessible writing style, albeit often doctrinaire in tone.[58] One *Landscape Architecture Quarterly* critic best described his style as "direct and business-like, with little attempt at literary finish or esthetic sentimentality."[59] Miller now applied his literary skill (and soon developed others, such as lecturing) as an assistant professor of landscape horticulture at the University of Illinois.[60] Miller's university colleague Charles Mulford Robinson (1869–1917), newly appointed professor of civic design, announced Miller's arrival in *Landscape Architecture Quarterly*, explaining that Miller, "of *The Garden Magazine*, was brought to take charge of the propagandist work in the state for 'the country beautiful.'"[61] In contrast to the European, neoclassical resonances of the City Beautiful, Miller's agrarian counterpart would draw upon more indigenous sources. The Country Beautiful, ideally, might "unite the spirit of ploughed land and prairie with the spirit of the city streets."[62]

Miller began a period of intense firsthand study aimed at familiarizing himself with local landscape design examples and interviewing their designers. An initial result of his study appeared only nine months after beginning his new post. In July 1913 the *Garden Magazine* reported that Miller's new home state was "ambitious to have an Illinois style of landscape gardening and is perhaps the first state consciously to conceive such an ideal."[63] For Miller, the country would be made beautiful not just through generic ornamental planting but by landscape gardening in an "Illinois style." Miller's launch of the new initiative actually enlarged the scope of this university enterprise. He imagined that his service to the agrarian constituency could become all-encompassing by means of local consultation, lectures, and exhibits. His proposal, in essence, called for the transformation of a lifestyle for an entire countryside. It was not, however, the result of consultation with Miller's colleagues. Eventually, Miller's quest for a holistic local style led to his undoing in academia.

In 1914 the university's Department of Horticulture consolidated its "propagandist work" in a new Division of Landscape Extension with Miller as its head. The division's formation was enabled by the passage of the national Smith-Lever Act. This

Figure 5. William E. Martin residence (1903) and gardens (ca. 1909) at Oak Park, Illinois. Frank Lloyd Wright, architect. Walter Burley Griffin, landscape architect. *Courtesy of the Martin family.*

progressivist act—one of the outcomes of Bailey's Country Life presidential commission initiatives—provided funding to land-grant universities for agricultural extension programs. Moreover, the Illinois division was pioneering. Miller himself reported that "Illinois was the first state to employ a man to give his entire time to landscape extension."[64] Under these auspices, he further defined and intensively promoted—via university publications, the horticultural press, and a popular series of lantern-slide lectures—a comprehensive awareness of the prairie and its potential for future landscape gardening (fig. 7).[65] He further expanded the scope of extension activities to include gratis landscape designs for Illinois citizens. For this purpose he assembled a staff of landscape architects to prepare designs for projects such as farmsteads, community parks, and street tree plantings (fig. 8).[66] Such designs were to serve as object lessons in beautification and stimulate popular interest in landscape gardening.

One of the first tangible outcomes of Miller's initiatives was *The "Illinois Way" of Beautifying the Farm*, published in 1914. Mirroring his Cornell technique, Miller advanced his landscape ideals via the university's long-established series of Agricultural Experiment Station circulars. Miller's circular, however, was a marked departure from its predecessors.[67] *The "Illinois Way"* was comparatively lengthy at thirty-three pages, more than double-sized in format, profusely illustrated, and thus more expensive to produce.

The circular's title reveals that Miller's focus was

novel. He now directly addressed the university's constituency, the citizens of the state. It is important to measure *The "Illinois Way"*'s contents against the backdrop of Miller's call for an Illinois style of landscape gardening. The establishment of this style, for Miller, was aligned with the parallel creation of a state style of architecture. In fact, a full-page illustration of the "Connecticut Style of Farm Architecture and Planting" precedes the Illinois text itself. In the

Figure 6. View of construction of Jens Jensen's garden additions to Frank Lloyd Wright's Midway Gardens (1914) at Chicago (1917). *Courtesy of The Morton Arboretum, Jens Jensen Collection in the Suzette Morton Davidson Special Collections.*

Figure 7. Wilhelm Miller's landscape extension "tools," a chest of lantern slides and an "inspirational" circular, *The "Illinois Way" of Beautifying the Farm*. From Miller, *Practical Help on Landscape Gardening*.

photograph caption, Miller explained that "Connecticut has many a clapboard farmhouse shaded by white-oaks or other trees that were here when the first white man came, while on the lawn may be a rhododendron or mountain laurel planted by the great-grandfather of the present owner." Miller next cited examples from Pennsylvania. Here he distinguished not state but "county styles" of "farm architecture and planting."[68] Lancaster County was to be identified by its "brick houses with double porches, quaint projections on the roof to prevent snowslides, and a 'date stone,'" and Delaware County by farmhouses of "native stone." The majority of Miller's prototypes were historical ones drawn from the eastern half of the nation. The distribution of these farmhouses, however,

was not a function of county or state boundaries. To the contrary, the dwellings more often architecturally inscribed original patterns of land settlement. Use of local building materials correlated more with availability in a given locale than with stylistic intent. Miller's reliance upon these archaic examples belies an implicit assumption that Illinois lacked such a patina of colonial antiquity and effectively remained, even in the twentieth century, a frontier. Moreover, despite inclusion of the term "planting" in his stylistic labels, he only incidentally mentions a handful of distinctive tree species. Here it is architecture—not gardens—that figures most prominently as expressive of "state style." Miller's attention to architecture, however, is conceptually important; that the farmhouse was a fundamental unit in the larger rural landscape compelled the landscape horticulture professor to now include architecture within his critical gaze. *The "Illinois Way"* revealed that architecture was Miller's stylistic barometer and he now sought its vegetal analogue.

Despite an emphasis on the horticultural content of gardens, *The "Illinois Way"* was not devoid of stylistic revelation. Hints at what would later emerge as Miller's prairie style pervaded the document. For instance, a photograph of a house by Spencer, replete with a garden by Jensen, was featured on the cover. Miller included this work as an example of his preferred style of farm architecture and gardening; he neglected to inform his readers, however, that this was not a farmstead but a suburban estate. Miller explained in the cover caption that the house was "built on horizontal lines, to repeat

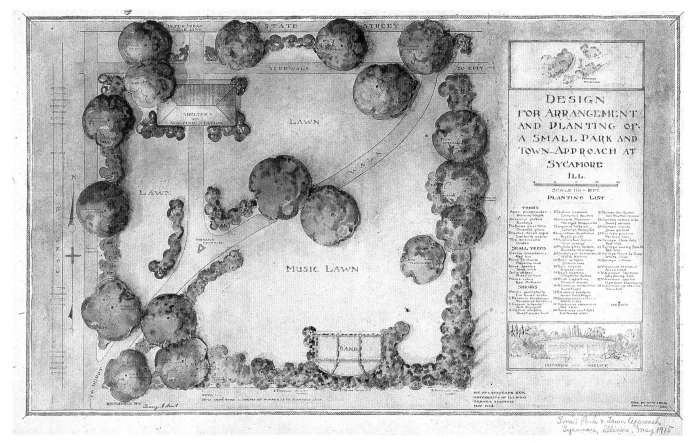

Figure 8. "Design for Arrangement and Planting of a Small Park and Town Approach at Sycamore, Ill." (1915). Franz Aust, landscape architect (for the Division of Landscape Extension, University of Illinois). *Courtesy of the State Historical Society of Wisconsin.*

the great horizontal lines of the prairie."[69] In the text he noted that Jensen's hawthorn plantings were "for the same purpose" and that Spencer's and Jensen's work was "of a new and virile school of western art."[70] He listed Sullivan and Wright also as architects of this school (although he did not illustrate their work), and in landscape gardening Jensen and Simonds. Enigmatically, Miller informed his readers only that "these men no longer fear or despise the prairie; they love it, and are opening our eyes to its true wonder and beauty." He again mentioned that "horizontal lines are fundamental in the new western or prairie school of architecture and landscape gardening." Apart from native plants, Miller offered only one example of a design feature that stylistically distinguished his "Illinois Way": Jensen's prairie river at Chicago's Humboldt Park. This feature was illustrated in the circular, and Miller explained in the caption that "the famous 'prairie river'" included "a miniature cataract modeled after those in the [local] Rock River and a bank full" of prairie flowers. Save for this, Miller provided few clues as to what specifically distinguished the work of the "new" and "virile" school.

He saved his greatest revelation until the conclusion, an inspirational manifesto entitled "The Religion of the Prairie." In contrast to the pragmatism of his opening passage—"Nobody can afford to have bare and ugly home grounds. It is bad business"[71]—he ended with "The greatest race the world shall ever know will be cradled in the Middle West."[72] Miller did not theoretically realize his aim of a state style of gardening in The "Illinois Way." Instead, the circular was more a polemic urging the use of native Illinois plants than it was an exposition of new stylistic technique. Perhaps owing to Jensen's influence, though, Miller would soon abandon the political boundary of the state for an ecological one, the prairie region.

In October 1914, only months after The "Illinois Way," Miller published his second circular. The two could not be more different. The latter document is accurately described by its title, Practical Help on Landscape Gardening: How to Get Illustrated Lectures, Advice, and Plans for Home Grounds, Streets, Roads, Library, School, and Other Public Grounds. It was half the size and length of its predecessor and largely devoid of inspirational content. One surmises that Miller's university colleagues, if not his agricultural audience, were not sympathetic to his secular "religion of the prairie." Might the Practical Help circular also have been Miller's counter-gesture—perhaps mandated by his superiors—of concern that The "Illinois Way" was overly inspirational?

The Prairie Spirit in Landscape Gardening was published in November 1915, three years after Miller's move to Illinois. The Prairie Spirit marked not only the achievement of his philosophical and aesthetic quest for an American style but also the emergence of a literally applied prairie style. In this document, Miller defined the "prairie style" as

> a new mode of design and planting, which aims to fit the peculiar scenery, climate, soil, labor and other conditions of the prairies, instead of copying literally the manners and materials of other regions. . . . [The prairie style is] characterized by preservation of typical western scenery, by restoration of local color [native vegetation], and by repetition of the horizontal line of land or sky which is the strongest feature of prairie scenery. (5)

Miller's effort to formulate a regional aesthetic gained resolution and maturity from his contact with Jens Jensen, who provided Miller with a conceptual design vocabulary for the prairie style, derived from his own work, and introduced Miller to his novel application of plant ecology. Miller now fused his advocacy of

native plants and "nature-like" compositions with a distinctly regional landscape and plant ecology. The science of plant ecology, for North America, had been almost single-handedly developed by Henry C. Cowles (1869–1939) at the University of Chicago. Cowles became first Jensen's and then Miller's friend.[73] Together, Miller and Jensen set out to imbue landscape gardening with Cowles's ecological thought. For Miller and Jensen, the application of ecology to landscape design depended fundamentally on the concept of the "plant society" or "association." Describing ecology as "a new and fascinating branch of botany," Miller cited Cowles's work and defined plant societies as "combinations of plants that are far more effective . . . than any which can be invented by man, because Nature has evolved them by ages of experiment" (18, 23).

While the concept of "plant societies" could be literally applied to landscape gardening, it also allowed Miller's and Jensen's landscape approach to be expanded to an even greater scale. They came to view the Illinois landscape through an ecological lens, systematically classifying it into scenery types such as "prairie," "lake bluff," and "ravine," analogous to whole plant societies (12).[74] The most distinctive and characteristic elements of each scenery or landscape type were next to be defined. Foremost would be the prairie rivers, striated rock outcrops, and "stratified" plants (that is, those characterized by a horizontal branching habit, such as the hawthorn). Use of the latter enabled designers to "repeat the line of the prairie" in a manner akin to the Prairie School architects' use of ribbons of casement windows, deep roof overhangs, and terrace or garden projections (19–21).

It was Jens Jensen who earliest translated these landscape elements into a unique design vocabulary. In both his domestic and his public park designs, he incorporated meandering watercourses, their margins defined by striated rockwork and lushly planted with vegetation that was ecologically appropriate (to the scenery type if not the actual site). Open lawns—metaphorical prairies—were enclosed and defined with stratified plants. Ultimately, for Jensen and Miller alike, landscape design, metaphorically shaped out of the local landscape materials, could reveal and affirm the latent indigenous order of the larger regional landscape.

Once all these crucial landscape elements had been discerned and restated, Miller concluded that "all prairie scenery [can] be reduced to two units, the broad view and the long view" (17). Miller defined the "broad view" as "the one that suggests infinity and power and is more inspiring for occasional visits." The "long view"—as exemplified in Simonds's constructions at Graceland Cemetery—"is more human and intimate, and often more satisfactory to live with." These viewpoints (in reality, control artifices for landscape design) were to be defined and accentuated by foreground plantings of indigenous trees and shrubs. The immensity and openness of the prairie required much from plantings. Through the creation of such views, the "fearful Infinite could be transformed into the friendly finite" (21). Miller reduced the boundless prairie landscape into a series of controllable and comprehensible vignettes, enabling the viewer to establish his psychological place by means of a carefully determined foreground. These key concepts of the long and broad views were Miller's unique contribution.

The majority of Miller's text and images is given over to Jensen's examples; in fact, The Prairie Spirit documents Jensen's approach as much as it does Miller's. Perhaps owing to this, and lest he be seen as effectively advertising the work of only a single person, Miller promoted the notion of a collective "Prairie School."[75] As he had done the year before in The "Illinois Way," Miller paired Jensen with Simonds. The Prairie Spirit, however, revealed that the ranks of the school had swelled in the interim. Here, for the first time,

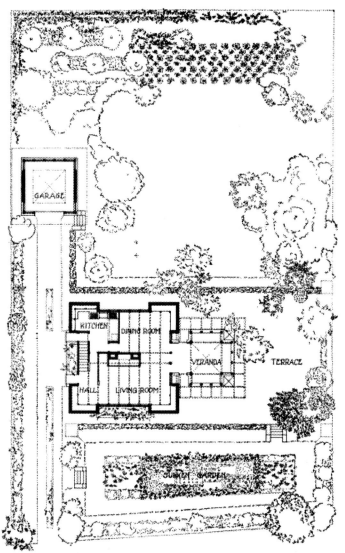

Figure 9. Plan of first floor and grounds of Harry E. Gunn residence (1911, razed) at Tracy (now Chicago), Illinois. Walter Burley Griffin, architect and landscape architect. From H.V. Von Holst, *Modern American Homes* (Chicago, 1912).

Miller promotes Walter Burley Griffin as a new exponent of the prairie style. Also members are "several [unidentified] young men whose work is promising" (3). Miller does admit, however, that landscape gardeners "who acknowledge the prairie as a leading motive in their work" are "not numerous" (3).

The inclusion of Simonds is not surprising, as Miller had regularly promoted his work in print. But Simonds did not care to be included. In his review of Miller's draft manuscript, the senior Chicago landscape gardener declared that Miller's terms "Prairie Spirit" and "Prairie Style" "do not appeal to me."[76] "Of course," Simonds continued, "I love the prairie and I think Illinois is a beautiful state. It is not essentially different, however, from Iowa and Indiana." Not only did Simonds reject the existence of "a distinct 'Prairie Style,'" he also explained that he "paid no attention to any so-called style" in his own work. Rather, he did whatever would "make the most beautiful effect."

Bryan Lathrop, Simonds's mentor and patron, was even harsher in his criticism.[77] Lathrop thought Miller's "prairie style" to be a conceit, and hoped that "there never will be one [prairie style], any more than that we shall have another American language in place

of the English language, or a body of American law which shall relegate the English common law to the scrap heap." In the end, Lathrop thought Miller's "deliberate attempt to form a new style" was mere fashion. Miller, in *The Prairie Spirit*, only partly addressed Simonds's and Lathrop's concerns. For instance, he credited Simonds as the founder not of the "Prairie School" but of a more ambiguous "middle western movement"—a role Simonds merited by his early use of native plants. Miller seems to have been largely undeterred by the criticism—perhaps owing to Jensen's enthusiastic support of his ideas.

If, as a recent assessment maintains, Simonds and his work have been eclipsed by the legacy of Jensen,[78] then the third designer of Miller's Prairie School troika—architect and landscape architect Walter Griffin—has been doubly eclipsed. Within landscape architecture Griffin is overshadowed by both Jensen and Simonds. And within architecture he continues to rest under the shadow of his former employer, Wright. *The Prairie Spirit* was the first public text, however, to feature Griffin's practice as a landscape architect. Griffin shared neither Miller's nor Jensen's pronounced advocacy of native plants nor the use of motifs such as Jensen's miniaturized prairie rivers. Although like Jensen an avid naturalist, Griffin in his extant design drawings reveals a liberal use of exotic vegetation and horticultural varieties in supplement to native plants, and his designs typically fused natural with formal elements (fig. 9).[79] Moreover, Griffin did not favor Miller's and Jensen's implicit boosterism of the prairie region. He left no written rhapsodies on the beauty of the prairie per se that might have confirmed his position as a regionalist. The design and accompanying text for Griffin's entry in the 1911 international competition for Australia's new federal capital city, Canberra, confirms a belief that his design stance was applicable far beyond the prairies. Pursuant to his victory in the competition, Griffin moved permanently to the distant antipodes in 1914, prior to the publication of *The Prairie Spirit*. Perhaps as yet unaware of the differences between Griffin's approach and his own, Miller solicited Griffin for photographs of his completed gardens. Upon considering the images, however, Miller informed Griffin that his gardens were not as "unconventional," as he hoped. "Strictly between you and me," he admonished Griffin, "[your work appears as though it] might have been done by Simonds, or even by any of the Eastern landscape gardeners, who have no conception of the prairie style of landscape gardening."[80] As in the case of Simonds's stylistically "conventional" landscapes, Miller apparently was placated by the fact that "as early as 1906 [Griffin] was using a high percentage of plants native to Illinois" (3). Miller's criticism also suggests that he held Jensen's work in highest esteem; that Griffin's work resembled Simonds's is a derogation.

Despite his stylistic reservations, Miller did not omit Griffin. He promoted him in word, if not image. Two other factors may have led Miller to include Griffin. Griffin then was a celebrity because of his winning the Canberra competition. (The heretofore little-known Chicagoan lectured on his prize-winning "Plans for a Capital City for Australia" at a 1913 national meeting of the American Society of Landscape Architects [ASLA] in New York City.)[81] Locally, Griffin's success was seen as a vindication of the Chicago School. Griffin's inclusion, therefore, may have been Miller's attempt to lend his own "Prairie School of Landscape Gardening" greater credibility and visibility, if only by association and reflection. Also, that Griffin was an architect and an alumnus of Miller's employer, the University of Illinois, was of particular significance to Miller. Though his gardens were too "conventional" for Miller's taste, Griffin's houses seamlessly fit the academic Miller's conception of "prairie style" architecture (fig. 10).

Figure 10. Harry E. Gunn residence. From H. V. Von Holst, *Modern American Homes* (Chicago, 1912).

"Conservation of native scenery" (6, 7), Miller's "first principle of the prairie style" is the most credible link among Simonds, Jensen, and Griffin. All were early participants in Chicago's conservation movement. Simonds and Jensen (and Dwight Perkins) were central figures in the establishment of Chicago's system of forest preserves. Beginning in 1908, five years before Miller's move to Illinois, Griffin, Jensen, and others, under the auspices of the Playground Association of Chicago (and later the Prairie Club), led Chicagoans on hikes through remnants of the rapidly vanishing native landscape with the view of stimulating interest in its conser-

vation. In 1913 Jensen even formed his own conservation organization, the Friends of Our Native Landscape (Miller was a charter member) (6) (fig. 11). Miller also lauded the Illinois work of landscape architect Warren H. Manning (1860–1938) in *The Prairie Spirit*, owing to Manning's initiative to conserve and restore the lake bluffs, north of Chicago (12). Although he did not inform his readers of the fact, Manning's practice was based not in the Middle West but in Boston.[82] The conservation movement was not a Prairie School novelty alone; it was a contemporaneous national phenomenon as well, one bound up in the reform ethos of Progressivism.

Putting aside the conceptual frame of Miller's Prairie School, his grouping of Simonds, Jensen, and Griffin is not without validity. All three designers did, in fact, know one another and were familiar with one another's work. Simonds, Griffin, and Miller, for instance, attended the first national meeting of the ASLA to be held in Chicago in 1913.[83] An even earlier instance of mutual awareness is that the young Griffin approached the elder Simonds for career advice prior to entering the University of Illinois in 1895.[84] Apparently dissatisfied with the lack of university curricula in landscape gardening at that time, Simonds urged Griffin to pursue architecture and study landscape gardening on his own, as he himself had done. Griffin heeded Simonds's advice, supplementing his study with the limited university classes relevant to landscape gardening. This regard of architecture as a portal into landscape gardening was an important bond between the two. Simonds, Griffin, and even Jensen—if only via Wright and architects in the same orbit—drew upon architectural thought as a premise for landscape design. Jensen and Griffin likewise shared an interest in civic design and urbanism, alternately serving as chairmen of the Chicago City Club's city planning committee. Both were members of the

Figure 11. Annual meeting of the Friends of Our Native Landscape at Warren's Woods, Three Oaks, Michigan (1914). Jens Jensen is in the back row, and Miller is standing to the right of center. *Courtesy of The Morton Arboretum, Jens Jensen Collection in the Suzette Morton Davidson Special Collections.*

Chicago Architectural Club, at least twice concurrently exhibiting their work in the annual club exhibition.[85] Jensen later ranked Griffin with Sullivan and Wright as a "master."[86]

There is no evidence, however, to suggest that the nature of the three men's professional association ever went beyond the collegial. Their relation mainly was born of their mutual pursuit of landscape design within close proximity of one another in Chicago, but they certainly did not perceive themselves as a collective school, "prairie" or otherwise. In fact, despite his rhetoric of a cohesive school, Miller actually saw Simonds and Jensen as rivals.[87]

If Miller's "Prairie School" was illusory or contrived, why did Simonds and Griffin permit their inclusion in *The Prairie Spirit*? Perhaps it was because the two subscribed to Miller's basic aims of stimulating popular interest in landscape gardening and conserving the native landscape. For Griffin, however, there would have been an additional, more pragmatic motivation. Anticipating only a three-year absence in Australia, he was endeavoring, in parallel, to keep his Chicago office open. Miller's notation that Griffin still "maintains an office in Illinois and undertakes new work in the Middle West" helped sustain Griffin's local visibility. In the end, however, Griffin closed the Chicago office in 1917 and never again resided in the United States. *The Prairie Spirit* marked one of the first—and last—times that Griffin's landscape architecture was called to the attention of an American audience.

As in *The "Illinois Way,"* Miller again included architecture within his critical purview. In *The Prairie Spirit* he included photographs of what he believed to be "prairie style" architecture, featuring the same house by Spencer with a Jensen garden on the circular's cover, albeit a different view. This time, Spencer's suburban house is classified as "a forerunner of a prairie type of permanent farm home." Land is to be directly associated with a house type. Only mentioned by name in the previous booklet, now Sullivan's and Wright's works are illustrated as well. And, inferring that the Prairie School had grown in the interim, Miller illustrated the work of William Drummond (1876–1946) for the first time. Through the inclusion of such architectural work, Miller was on his way to establishing landscape gardening as an integral component of a preexisting movement within architecture. By analogy, from arboriculture he was attempting to graft a promising branch onto an already established tree trunk. In this context Miller sought to supplant Tallmadge's "Chicago School" label—despite its currency—with the broadening term "Prairie School." Evidence for this comes from no less an authority than Frank Lloyd Wright. Saying that he was "unwilling to wear any tag which [would] identify [him] with any sect or system," Wright rejected Miller's nomenclature for, as he put it, "the 'school' you [Miller] would name."[88] (Given Miller's rural constituency, his motivation for the change of labels likely stemmed from the exclusively urban connotations of "Chicago.")

In Miller's view, Simonds's, Jensen's, and Griffin's work was inspired by and derived from the "prairie spirit," which was Miller's invocation of the power, security, and democratic values he believed to be inherent in the prairie landscape. These values were, he was convinced, fundamentally American ones. Unlike the prairie style, Miller intended the "prairie spirit" to be applied beyond the boundaries of Illinois or the region. He elaborated, revealing and shaping the potential for a national style:

> The prairie style ought not to be copied by people who live among the mountains or in the arid regions, simply because their friends in Illinois may have something beautiful in that style. The essence of landscape gardening is the accentuation of native scenery, and the

strong feature in mountainous countries is the vertical line, which mountaineers should repeat by planting their own aspiring evergreens, such as white spruce, hemlock, and balsam. (23)

Through the recognition and articulation of the "prairie spirit," Miller began to envision the emergence of a genuine and enduring American style. He had contended that the physical landscape of Europe, particularly the "complicated mountain systems," produced a "bewildering variety of languages, customs, and governments." Given the unifying presence of a common language, democratic government, and the perceived abundance of wide-open space, this unfortunate effect, he thought, should be avoided in America.

Miller's progressive, democratic ideals were fundamentally expressed in his aim that "everyone"—farmer and "city dweller" alike (2, 3, 10)—could participate in his movement. For Miller, even the "humblest renter" could "symbolize the prairie by putting a prairie rose beside the door" (2). Reminiscent of Downing, he argued that the "popular notion that landscape gardening is only for city parks and the wealthy few is a great mistake . . . so far as self-expression goes, landscape gardening offers as great an opportunity to every living soul as music does, or any other fine art" (10). His move to Illinois had been motivated by a desire to work with farmers and "those who can never afford to employ a landscape gardener." And he declared that agricultural landscape extension was the "democratic side of an art that has been too aristocratic."[89]

While attempting to establish democratic ideals, Miller and Jensen were also in favor of progressive social ideals. They tended to view the "wealthy elite"—the clientele of much landscape architecture at the time—with contempt. This bias is revealed in an exchange of letters among Miller, Jensen, and Frank Waugh in January 1916.[90] At this time, the three men were mutual friends and Waugh had just returned to Massachusetts after a visiting professorship at Illinois.[91] Their correspondence was precipitated by Miller's request that Jensen and Waugh review *The Prairie Spirit*. Like Miller and Jensen, Waugh advocated natural gardens, though as only one of a number of stylistic options available to the landscape architect. Waugh believed that every "well-trained landscape architect in America designs freely in either the formal or the natural style, frequently using both styles in different parts of the same project."[92] That Waugh was not as singularly committed to the natural garden as Jensen led to conflict.

Waugh summarized his criticism in a letter to Miller, who forwarded it to Jensen. In turn, and perhaps feeling that his own contributions of ideas to *The Prairie Spirit* were substantial, Jensen took it upon himself to respond directly. "Dear Brother Waugh," Jensen replied on 21 January 1916, "If you are willing to make gardens for society folks in harmony with their tastes; in other words, selling your soul, I shall have pity for you." The same day, Jensen wrote to Miller that Waugh "hasn't got the soul of an artist; he is willing to make gardens for rich society folks according to their demands, or as he states 'in harmony with their tastes.' God knows, as a rule, they havn't [sic] got any." "Dear Friend Jensen," Waugh replied three days later, "My theory is that a garden is not merely an artistic production in which I express my personality, but that it is a practical utility for my clients. Indeed I believe it is sound philosophy to place the requirements of my client first. If I can satisfy him and then afterward work out my artistic conceptions, so much the better." On 27 January Jensen confided to Miller that Waugh was "getting rattled . . . but I shall have no pity on him"; Waugh, Jensen jested, "must be chastised until his soul becomes pure." Jensen wrote Waugh the next day: "We have lots of people who think that because they have been able to acquire wealth they also have been able to acquire artistic taste. With the same air of superiority they rule their own employees. They think they can rule art and literature and dictate to the artist what they want him to do. This conceit of the rich American is not found anywhere else in the world."

A second bias of Miller and Jensen was that the Middle West was the most "American" section of the country. The two were not alone in this faith. Aside from architects such as Sullivan, contemporary author Hamlin Garland and others were advancing this view.[93] What was the source for this association of the prairies and "Americanism"? Actually, its origins can be traced at least to the late eighteenth century, when the Middle West (then known as the Northwest) constituted the American frontier. It was here that Thomas Jefferson wanted yeoman farmers to establish a new, agrarian, American society.[94] For Walt Whitman, too, the East in the late nineteenth century was too close socially and geographically to Europe and a feudal past. Whitman mused in *Specimen Days*: "I could not help thinking that it would be grander still to see all those inimitable American areas fused in the alembic of a perfect poem, or other aesthetic work, entirely western, fresh and limitless—altogether our own, without taste or trace of Europe's soil, reminiscence, technical letter or spirit." If only because of their removal at a great distance, the prairies offered promise as a remedy. As Richard Guy Wilson has noted, Whitman went so far as to prophesy "that a new man would arise out of the Western prairies—the American Adam, who would need a new art and architecture to create a new democratic society."[95] Sullivan, Wright, Griffin, and many of their middle western contemporaries embraced Whitman's writings, and, for them, "the prairie served as a metaphor, offering the promise of a new society and a new art, freed from stultified Old World and East Coast traditions." By 1918, as Wilson also notes, the Chicago architect Irving K. Pond observed that "the horizontal lines of the new expression appeal to the disciples of this [Prairie] school as echoing the spirit of the prairies of the great Middle West, which to them embodies the essence of democracy."[96]

What made the Middle West inherently democratic and American? For Miller, these attributes apparently were summed up in a single natural feature: landform. The very flatness of the land, with its omnipresent stretch to the horizon, was conducive to the development of democracy to its full potential. This flatness made the region the "runway of winds and ideas." "Between the Alleghenies and the Rockies . . . there are no mountain ranges . . . no barriers to human thought like the complicated mountain systems which have produced a bewildering variety of languages, customs, and governments in Europe."[97] At his most extreme, Miller, invoking Whitman's sentiments, contended that the "most creative people who ever lived were the Greeks, but the greatest race the world shall ever know will be cradled in the Middle West."[98] Ironically, though, much of the prairie by Miller's time already had been consumed by agriculture and urbanism. It was the concept of the prairies, not their actuality, that proved more powerful and enduring in the end.

Miller's third bias was one of design form. His prairie style implicitly derived from English picturesque naturalism as interpreted through American sources such as Downing, actually had little to do with a novel or alternative mode of design or style. Rather, it was distinguished by its horticultural program: the "prairie spirit" was to be fundamentally expressed through the direct use of plants native to the Middle West. In *The Prairie Spirit* Miller presupposed that the native vegetation he urged his readers to plant would be grouped in essentially naturalistic compositions.

He did briefly acknowledge that "the prairie style can be executed in the formal manner" (4), this assertion appearing as the caption for an illustration of a formal, symmetrically composed rose garden in Chicago's Humboldt Park (the only image of such a garden type in the entire circular). Miller explained that the designer, Jensen, "put hawthorns at the entrance to suggest the meeting of woods and prairie" and "lowered the garden two feet in order to get the flowers well below the level of the eye as they are on the prairie in the spring." (This rationale, though, was retrospective, as Jensen had designed the garden in 1907. The image perhaps appealed more for its symbolic value of the two large, iconic statues of bison flanking the entry and the prairie-style light standard—designed by architect Hugh Garden—visible in the background.)

By the time of *The Prairie Spirit*'s appearance in 1915 Miller and Jensen considered "nature-like," "pictorial" compositions of indigenous plants to be most appropriate to American democracy. For Miller, formal gardens were too rigid; Jensen was more emphatic, contending that the straight lines and formality of German gardens, for instance, reflected not democracy but a "craze for militarism." Costly to construct and maintain, formal gardens reflected not only the too-rigid alien European cultures, but also were too showy in their display of wealth.

The appeal of Miller's prototypical landscape ideal of an open lawn, framed and defined by masses of native vegetation—whether known as a lawn or "prairie"—is psychologically primal, tied to the concept of authenticity. "Nature-like" or "natural" compositions were supposedly authentic; formal or geometric compositions were "artificial" and mannered. This was how Miller had earlier distinguished Downing's "natural" style from the "artificial" gardens of the Italians and Dutch, and he again linked these ideas when he stated that "people generally pass in their appreciation from the temporary to the permanent, from the spectacular to the restful, from the showy to the quiet, from the artificial to the natural, from rare to common, from foreign to native" (32).[99]

In 1916 *The Prairie Spirit* was reviewed in *Landscape Architecture Quarterly*, the official organ of the ASLA. For the anonymous reviewer, Miller's prairie style, rather than being in itself new or American, was little more than a variant of the more timeless principles of the natural style. Moreover, the chief weakness of Miller's hybrid style was its limited application; it would "succeed fully," the reviewer asserted, "only where the natural landscape is dominant." In advancing this view, the critic isolated Miller's single example of the formal, symmetrical prairie style, Jensen's Humboldt Park rose garden. The "prairie style here," the reviewer observed, "seems, to say the most of it, a bit dilute!"[100] The review did conclude, however, on a more positive note. From the professional perspective, the reviewer wrote, Miller was essentially "telling the people of Illinois that they have in their landscape an asset in beauty worth preserving, and he is showing them, actually and practically, good ways to go about to preserve it." For Miller, though, the reviewer had missed all his key points: absent was any recognition of what he believed to be the style's progressive, democratic underpinnings or even that his audience was primarily rural. In reaction, Miller wrote to Jensen:

> Since you and Frank [Waugh] are the only two persons in captivity who dislike 'Landscape Architecture' [Quarterly] I am writing you the joyous news that the 'Harvard Chill' which I have been expecting by pipe line direct from the North Pole has finally arrived by the Boston Refrigerator Express. . . . I expect that you will both take a furtive peak at somebody else's copy in order to join in the merry Ha! Ha! at my expense.[101]

So far as Miller was concerned, it was the eastern domination of the magazine, and, more broadly, of the profession of landscape architecture, that explained this lack of sympathy for his middle western ideals.

A more sympathetic review came from without the landscape profession, from *The Architectural Record*.[102] Therein, elder Chicago architect and critic Peter B. Wight (1838–1925) reported that Miller's "remarkable pamphlet" was "one of the natural results of his study of landscape art, horticulture, and arboriculture. He perceived the influence of the prairie on the design of many buildings, the erection of which had come under his observation, and he bore witness to it."[103] It was not so much the alleged stylistic novelty of Miller's landscape school that appealed to Wight; for him, Miller's achievement lay more in the efforts to align his school of landscape gardening with its architectural counterpart. "It is gratifying to know," Wight concluded, "that an educational movement is on foot to harmonize the landscape treatment of this great area with what the architects have been doing." For Wight, Miller—from the vantage point of a latecomer to the Chicago scene—had fused heretofore seemingly disparate works from two professions into a logical collective whole.

The University of Illinois did not share Wight's favorable view. In fact, *The Prairie Spirit* proved to be Miller's swan song. The university sought peer assessment of Miller's circular, shortly after its appearance. To this end, J. Horace McFarland (1859–1948) was contacted. Although the noted civic authority believed the document to be an "important contribution," McFarland conceded that it might, as the university suspected, "be slightly . . . in advance of the present absorptive capacity of your people."[104] As perhaps first signaled by the *Practical Help* circular, Miller had apparently gone too far with the "inspirational stuff."[105] Moreover, an assessment by Karl Lohmann, in 1922, suggests that Miller's production of landscape designs also had proven a problematic aspect of his landscape extension activities.[106] That these designs were prepared gratis raised professional resistance and heightened the potential for conflict between the university and practicing landscape architects. This enterprise was also expensive, and not only in financial resources; travel throughout Illinois to lecture and consult with the division's rural "clientele" consumed increasingly inordinate amounts of time.

Unfortunately for Miller, the university's apprehensions about his work coincided with its dramatically reduced funding in the midst of World War I. It decided to disband its infant Division of Landscape Extension. Miller was informed that his contract would not be renewed when it ended in September 1916.[107] But Miller's activities already had proven influential. About the time *The Prairie Spirit* appeared, Miller's chief designer Franz Aust (1885–1963) took up a new position at the University of Wisconsin, and he used Miller's landscape extension techniques as a template for his own.[108]

One of Miller's last publications before leaving the university appeared in the February 1916 garden issue of *The Minnesotan*.[109] Here he revised a synopsis of *The Prairie Spirit* as "The Minnesota Spirit in Landscape Gardening." As part of his new geographical focus, Miller attempted to promote Minneapolis architects William Gray Purcell (1880–1965) and George Grant Elmslie (1871–1952).[110] This shift of attention to Minnesota raises the possibility that Miller was interested in relocating there, but more importantly, Miller's article confirms his belief that his "prairie spirit" approach was elastic enough even to accommodate a more sylvan, rolling terrain.

A month later Miller renewed his contact with Frank Lloyd Wright, advising him about the design of the terrace gardens included in Wright's design for the Imperial Hotel at Tokyo. Wright "seems to like many of my suggestions," Miller wrote to his poet friend Vachel Lindsay.[111] According to Miller, Wright was "visibly blending the two civilizations [East and West] in the building's exterior," and Miller had thought the garden design should do the same. Although nothing apparent resulted from Miller's consultation, the episode foreshadowed Miller's next career move.

Confronted with the expiration of his Illinois contract, Miller elected to enter directly into the practice of landscape architecture. His decision to redirect his career, like Jensen's, came relatively late in life. He was nearly fifty. Given his lack of experience and the diminished prospects of new work in a world that was now at war, it would be difficult to imagine a less opportune time to establish a practice. Nonetheless, Miller opened a professional office in Chicago's Steinway Hall in October 1916.[112] Although no longer a haven for Prairie School architects by then, Steinway Hall did remain the locus of Jensen's landscape practice.[113]

Only about a month into Miller's practice, *The Architectural Record* solicited him for his "creed." This request was triggered by a negative reaction to *The Prairie Spirit*, as reviewed in the October issue. Miller complied, asserting that his was "not an academic creed, for I have left the university life and am now practicing what I preach."[114] The creed in its entirety offers insight into his design thinking as a landscape architect, but the opening and closing statements are the most salient here. Concern for nation—not region—surges forth in Miller's opening tenet: "I believe that one of the greatest assets any country can have is a national style of architecture and landscape architecture." In closing, Miller asserted "that the prairie style of landscape architecture is the first successful attempt in America to develop a style of gardening based upon scenery of a well-marked, natural region." Miller's creed, however, became his coda: he would leave Chicago within months and retire completely within four years.

Apart from its short duration, little is known of the scale and scope of Miller's Chicago practice. One apparent project, however, has come to light. In the 1950s Miller's Minnesota acquaintance, architect William Purcell, remembered Miller as a landscape architect collaborator with his firm and thought that Miller might have designed the garden for the Amy Hamilton Hunter house at Flossmoor, Illinois (fig. 12), designed by Purcell's Chicago partner and former Sullivan associate George Elmslie in 1916.[115] Even if Purcell's memory was faulty in regard to an actual commission, his remark nonetheless suggests that Miller, no longer the academic or writer, now sought to establish professional relations with his heretofore only literary associates.[116]

In parallel with—or perhaps as a part of—his attempt to establish a professional practice, Miller continued to publish articles, albeit far fewer in number. In March 1917 he published another article in *The Minnesotan*.[117] The article, however, was archaic, evocative of his turn-of-the-century writings. He merely urges the people of Minnesota to avoid the "bedding system" of the "gardenesque style" in favor of the "landscape style" and the use of native plants. The text lacks any reference to the Prairie School. This absence, coupled with the fact that his byline title was "Landscape Architect," raises the possibility that Miller saw the essay as an advertisement for his new practice; perhaps he was aware that his Prairie School proselytizing might preclude certain clientele. All of Miller's other known articles from this period, published under the title "Landscape Architect," are devoid of his Prairie School rhetoric.[118]

Indeed, the start of his Chicago practice coincided with the

Figure 12. Amy Hamilton Hunter residence (1917) at Flossmoor, Illinois. George Grant Elmslie, Purcell and Elmslie, architect. Wilhelm Miller, landscape architect (?). *Courtesy of the Northwest Architectural Archives.*

composition. Spatially, the plantings were segregated to form areas labeled "The Meadow," "The Lawn," and a "Wild Garden." Within this "nature-like" frame, Miller also inserted a rectilinear "Vegetable Garden" and a "Rustic Summer House." As with his writings of the period, the drawing is devoid of prairie style nomenclature, and a careful reading of the plan suggests that Miller was no longer practicing what he preached. This was a conventional garden, similar to those of "Eastern landscape gardeners, who have no conception of the prairie style of landscape gardening."

By 1919 Miller had formed a partnership with Charles A. Tirrell (1883–192?), a graduate of Frank Waugh's course at the University of Massachusetts and a former "head" man in Jensen's office.[123] Together they began practice as "Miller and Tirrell, Landscape Architects."[124] Miller's need for a partner likely was not motivated by the demands of a burgeoning number of commissions; every indication is that he was perpetually struggling to maintain the practice. But partnership with Tirrell seems to have brought a wealth of professional experience to the office. One of Miller's Detroit employees, Harlow O. Whittemore, recollected that Miller received a large-scale commission in 1919: "the landscape development of an entire new city, 'Marysville' on the St. Claire River" in Michigan.[125] Marysville was conceived by C. Harold Wills as a model industrial community for workers at his new Wills St. Claire automobile factory.[126] Although the layout of an entire town was beyond Miller's abilities, it would not have exceeded Tirrell's competency. The exact nature of Miller's involvement in the design and construction of Marysville is unclear. A 20 June 1919 news-

incremental demise of the Prairie School, at least within architecture. In April 1917, less than six months after Miller's office opened, there were indications that the mood in Chicago had changed. That month Thomas Tallmadge, in a review of the annual Chicago Architectural Club exhibition, lamented, "Where are Sullivan, Wright, Griffin and the others? The absence of work of these men has removed from the show the last vestige of local color."[119] For Miller, the impending dissolution of the Prairie School was likely as perplexing as it was disheartening. "On the eve of the First World War," David Van Zanten wrote, several events—most prominently Griffin's international competition victory—"all gave the semblence [sic] of a burst of creative energy."[120] For Miller's Prairie School, however, it was a false dawn.

Apparently unsuccessful in Chicago, Miller shifted his practice to hometown Detroit in 1917.[121] Only one drawing has come to light to document his designs: a planting plan dated October 1917 for a domestic garden at Madison, Wisconsin (fig. 13).[122] The circumstances of the commission are unknown; the design consists predominantly (but not exclusively) of native vegetation, organized in—using Miller's early terminology—a "nature-like," "pictorial"

paper confirms that "landscape architect Miller, of Detroit" had been "entrusted in a general way with the landscaping of the new city . . . [and] before long his ideas will begin to crystallize in a layout of the new industrial town."[127] No other documentation specifically attributing the actual design of the town plan to Miller or Tirrell, however, has surfaced.

The commission for Marysville likely bolstered the firm, yet Miller's practice deteriorated further. Whittemore believed that Miller "did not know very much about the practice of landscape architecture but he had employed two men from Jensen's office who were very good."[128] Despite Tirrell's and his unidentified cohorts' presence, Whittemore did not "think his business was successful for long as people did not have confidence in him." In addition to Miller's lack of experience, other immediate conditions may have weighed against him. The anti-German sentiments engendered by World War I prompted him to change his given name in 1918 from "Wilhelm" to "William"; with the war only recently ended, perhaps the demand for new work had yet to resume. Furthermore, personal tensions had arisen between the two partners.[129] Collectively, these circumstances undermined

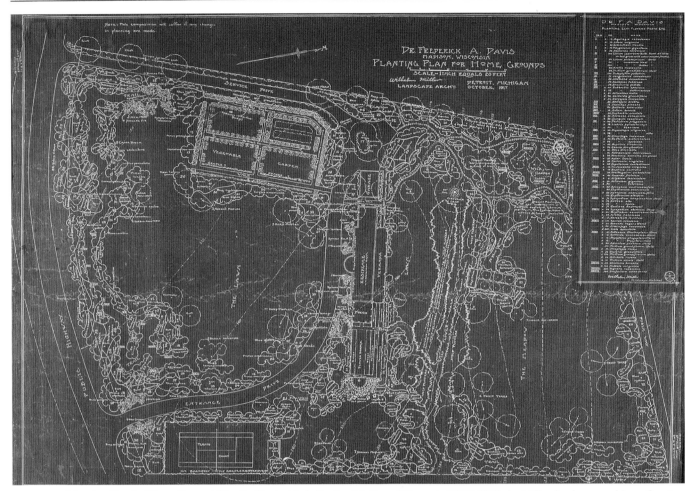

Figure 13. "Planting Plan for Home Grounds" for Dr. Frederick A. Davis at Madison, Wisconsin (1917). Wilhelm Miller, landscape architect. *Courtesy State Historical Society of Wisconsin.*

Miller's efforts to maintain his firm, and the practice closed in 1920. Tirrell returned to Chicago and "William" Miller retired to Los Angeles, California.

Shortly after his move to California, Miller immersed himself, with characteristic zeal, in the flora of the new environs. In December 1920 he published a listing of "Shrubs and Vines for California Gardens" in *The Garden Magazine*, the journal for which he had been founding editor fifteen years prior.[130] Therein the plant selection criterion of "Shrubs that Blend with the Native Landscape" is the only allusion to his long advocacy of the native landscape as a design source. This article appears to have been Miller's last. His sister-in-law, naturalist Julia Ellen Rogers, one of the few sources on his later years, reported that "extension work in the University of California, planting and care of a young cherry orchard at Beaumont" filled Miller's last years.[131] Miller continued to correspond with Wright and Jensen; his last surviving letter to Jensen is dated only months before his death.[132] Wilhelm Tyler Miller died on 16 March 1938.

In 1922, about two years after Miller left the region, Thomas Tallmadge again assessed the middle western scene. Having detected in 1917 that the once-pervasive influence of Sullivan, Wright, and Griffin was already much diminished, Tallmadge now concluded that "the effort to create an American style [of architecture] has proved a failure."[133] Instead, East Coast eclecticism now domi-

nated the region. The architect lamented that many middle western houses had become "so cosmopolitan in type that each could have smiled forth just as confidently from among the maples of Newport or the laurels of Fiesole."[134]

Tallmadge continued his postmortem with an examination of the region's gardens. "If sameness of type is a defect," the architect bleakly judged, then "our gardens are in worse case than our country houses."[135] Tallmadge then sketched out what, for him, was "the only national style of gardening we ever had," one which "flourished fifty years ago": "The hard smooth lawn, the canna and geranium flower beds cunningly fashioned by the German gardener in the shape of stars, crescents, anchors, etc.; the cast iron dog; the bright green fountain with the white storks of the same rigid material as the dog and drooling a stream of water as feeble and futile as the whole layout." Tallmadge's list of definitive features evoked Miller's aesthetic nemesis, the "scattered" gardenesque style; Miller could not have written a better description himself. This sort of gardenesque "national garden," Tallmadge said, was "fortunately gone."

Were Miller's four years of Illinois extension activities influential in this erasure? Apparently not. "No," Tallmadge continued, "the principal defect of landscape gardening in the Middle West is that there is so little of it." There was, however, one important exception to the dismal state of the region's gardens: "the profusion of beautiful gardens in [suburban] Lake Forest, Illinois," to the north of Chicago. Here Tallmadge discerned the "considerable and beneficial influence of Jens Jensen—an apostle of natural planting and informal arrangement, and of the development of the 'Prairie Line'"—as the sole surviving agent. In architecture, the earlier influence of Sullivan, Wright, and others was collective. In contrast, the influence in garden design now appeared highly singular. No mention was made of Miller, or of regional labels—save for the "Prairie Line" acknowledgment. Only Jensen's influence seems to have endured. Jensen continued to actively practice landscape architecture well into the Depression-ridden 1930s, until retiring to Wisconsin to establish his own school of landscape architecture, "The Clearing."

Nevertheless, the moment in which Jensen and Miller worked had provided a new impulse. Remnants of the indigenous, presettlement landscape—features securely familiar to a population very lately of rural origin, only then becoming an urban one— were being destroyed at an alarming rate. Explosive urban and suburban growth gave rise to a country-life imperative, reflected in and supported by magazines such as *Country Life in America* and *The Garden Magazine*. (Ironically, this growth also provided Jensen's

and Wright's clientele.) In his 1900 review of Wright's architecture, Robert Spencer did not fail to note that "from the farms . . . a tide of vigorous youth pours into the cities." In assessing the popularity of his "American garden," Jensen noted that the urban Chicagoans "exclaimed excitedly when they saw [native wild] flowers they recognized [and] welcomed them as they would a friend from home."[136]

Such potent, nostalgic reactions became Miller's and Jensen's catalysts to make conservation of the native landscape the absolute touchstone of the prairie style. Their urgent conservation advocacy—as recorded in *The Prairie Spirit*—was both a eulogy for the older, stronger bonds between people and their soil, and a prophecy of the diminishing direct contact in cities with the earth. As witnesses to America's transformation from an agrarian to an urban, industrial society, Wilhelm Miller and Jens Jensen saw the progressive ideals of "country life" as being equally applicable to the city. In their vision, the native landscape—whether vestigially conserved or re-created by design—was the civilizing agent in the development of a new, modern society.

NOTES

Christopher Vernon is Senior Lecturer in Landscape Architecture at The University of Western Australia.

The present essay was partially derived from a paper presented at the 1994 Studies in Landscape Architecture symposium at Dumbarton Oaks, "Nature and Ideology: Natural Garden Design in the Twentieth Century." See also my "Wilhelm Miller and 'The Prairie Spirit' in Landscape Gardening," in *Regional Garden Design in the United States*, ed. Therese O'Malley and Marc Trieb (Washington, D.C.: Dumbarton Oaks Research Library and Collection, 1995), 271–75, and "Wilhelm Miller: Prairie Spirit in Landscape Gardening," in *Midwestern Landscape Architecture*, ed. William H. Tishler (Urbana: University of Illinois Press, 2000), 174–92. I extend special thanks to my mentor, Dr. Walter L. Creese, for his review of an earlier version of this essay and especially for his continuing inspiration and encouragement. Thanks also to Melanie Simo, Leonard Eaton, and Donald Leslie Johnson for their support and comments on the manuscript. I have also gained much from ongoing dialogue with Robert Grese on the work of Jens Jensen.
Note: parenthetical in-text page references are to *The Prairie Spirit in Landscape Gardening*.

1. Grant Carpenter Manson, *Frank Lloyd Wright to 1910: The First Golden Age* (New York: Reinhold, 1958), 102. Manson was the first to comprehensively analyze Wright's prairie oeuvre. For Manson's own account of his classic study, see Grant Carpenter Manson, "The Wonderful World of Taliesin: My Twenty Years on Its Fringes," *Wisconsin Magazine of History* 73, no. 1 (Autumn 1989): 33–41. Standard references on the period include Mark L. Peisch, *The Chicago School of Architecture: Early Followers of Sullivan and Wright* (New York: Random House, 1964), esp. chap. 6, and H. Allen Brooks, *The Prairie School: Frank Lloyd Wright and His Midwest Contemporaries* (Toronto: University of Toronto Press, 1972). Peisch and Brooks also cite Miller's circular.

2. On Jensen, see Leonard K. Eaton's pioneering study, *Landscape Artist in America: The Life and Work of Jens Jensen* (Chicago: University of Chicago Press, 1964), and "Jens Jensen Reconsidered," in Eaton, *Gateway Cities and Other Essays* (Ames: Iowa State University Press, 1989), 129–41. Also see the following works by Robert E. Grese: *Jens Jensen: Maker of Natural Parks and Gardens* (Baltimore: Johns Hopkins University Press, 1992); "The Prairie Gardens of O. C. Simonds and Jens Jensen," in *Regional Garden Design in the United States*, ed. Therese O'Malley and Marc Trieb (Washington, D.C.: Dumbarton Oaks Research Library and Collection,

1995), 99–123; and "Jens Jensen: The Landscape Architect and Conservationist," in *Midwestern Landscape Architecture*, ed. William H. Tishler (Urbana: University of Illinois Press, 2000), 117–41. On Simonds, see Mara Gelbloom, "Ossian Simonds: Prairie Spirit in Landscape Gardening," *Prairie School Review* 12, no. 2 (1975): 15–18; Walter L. Creese, "Graceland Cemetery and the Landscaped Lawn," in his *The Crowning of the American Landscape: Eight Great Spaces and Their Buildings* (Princeton: Princeton University Press, 1985), 205–18; and Julia Sniderman Bachrach, "Ossian Cole Simonds: Conservation Ethic in the Prairie Style," in Tishler, *Midwestern Landscape Architecture*, 80–98.

3. One wonders if it was Wright himself or perhaps Marion Mahony Griffin, architect wife of Walter Burley Griffin (whom Manson interviewed), who called Manson's attention to Miller's circular. Rediscovery of Miller's document has in turn facilitated the burgeoning popularity of Jensen's and Simonds's works.

4. Wilhelm Miller, "What Is the Matter with Our Water Gardens?," *Country Life in America* 22, no. 4 (15 June 1912): 54.

5. This and other biographical information is included in Miller's Deceased Alumni file, Rare and Manuscript Collections, Carl A. Kroch Library, Cornell University (hereafter cited as DAF). Also valuable is his sister-in-law Julia Ellen Rogers's obituary [*Wilhelm Miller:*] *His Life Story* (1938), Staff file, University Archives, University of Illinois at Urbana-Champaign (hereafter cited as SF). As reflected in its glowing prose, Rogers's essay was intended as a tribute and must be read with caution.

6. SF, 1. On Tyler, see Alexander Moore, "Moses Coit Tyler," in *Dictionary of Literary Biography: American Historians, 1866–1912*, vol. 47, ed. Clyde N. Wilson (Detroit: Gale Research Company, 1986), 317–25.

7. SF, 1. Miller discovered that Jensen and Waugh both believed music to be a potent inspirational source for landscape design.

8. Ibid.

9. Wilhelm Miller, dedication in *What England Can Teach Us about Gardening* (New York: Doubleday, Page, 1911), n.p. Documentation of Miller's Cornell studies is found in his Graduate School Records file, Rare and Manuscript Collections, Carl A. Kroch Library, Cornell University. On Bailey, see Andrew Denny Rodgers III, *Liberty Hyde Bailey: A Story of American Plant Sciences* (Princeton: Princeton University Press, 1949), and Grese's entry on Bailey in *Pioneers of American Landscape Design*, ed. Charles A. Birnbaum and Robin Karson (New York: McGraw-Hill, 2000), 6–8.

10. Wilhelm Miller, "Chrysanthemums at Cornell University," *Garden and Forest* 8, no. 404 (20 November 1895): 466. He continued to publish in

Garden and Forest until it ceased publication in 1897. For other early pieces in *Garden and Forest* on flowers, see bibliography.

11. Articles about landscape architecture regularly appeared in *Garden and Forest*. The journal also included middle western items; Olmsted's Chicago work, for example, was reported and illustrated in "The Revised Plan for Jackson Park, Chicago," 9, no. 430 (20 May 1896): 201–5. Also see O. C. Simonds's "The Landscape Gardener and His Work," 10, no. 491 (21 July 1897): 282–83.

12. *A Talk about Dahlias*, Cornell University Agricultural Experiment Station Bulletin no. 128 (February 1897): 113. It is likely that Miller adopted Bailey's own views on gardens; see L. H. Bailey, "What Are the Fundamental Concepts in Landscape Gardening?," *Park and Cemetery* 7, no. 10 (December 1897): 226.

13. L. H. Bailey, ed., and Wilhelm Miller, assoc. ed., *Cyclopedia of American Horticulture: Comprising Suggestions for Cultivation of Horticultural Plants, Descriptions of the Species of Fruits, Vegetables, Flowers and Ornamental Plants Sold in the United States and Canada, together with Geographical and Biographical Sketches*, 4 vols. (New York: Macmillan, 1900–1902).

14. Wilhelm Miller to Dr. Sherrill, 3 August 1898, Liberty Hyde Bailey Papers, Rare and Manuscript Collections, Carl A. Kroch Library, Cornell University (hereafter cited as Bailey MSS).

15. Ibid.

16. "Downing, Andrew Jackson," *Cyclopedia*, vol. 2, 501–2.

17. See, for example, L. H. Bailey, Wilhelm Miller, and C. E. Hunn, *The 1895 Chrysanthemums*, Cornell University Agricultural Experiment Station Bulletin no. 112 (February 1896); L. H. Bailey and Wilhelm Miller, *Chrysanthemums of 1896*, Bulletin no. 136 (May 1897); and Wilhelm Miller, *Fourth Report Upon Chrysanthemums*, Bulletin no. 147 (April 1898).

18. L. H. Bailey, preface to Miller, *A Talk about Dahlias*, 100.

19. "American Country Life and Art," *Architectural Record* 11 (1902): 112.

20. In *How to Make a Flower Garden: A Manual of Practical Information and Suggestions*, ed. Wilhelm Miller (New York: Doubleday, Page, 1903), 52.

21. Vol. 4, no. 5 (September 1903): 349–50.

22. Miller, *What England Can Teach*. The book also was published in England as *The Charm of English Gardens* (London: Hodder and Stoughton, 1911), with a preface by the celebrated garden designer Gertrude Jekyll. Jekyll observed that "to persons of refined taste in England, it would seem most fitting that a national style of gardening for America should develop on 'Colonial' lines."

23. For a moving account of his meeting with Jensen, see Wilhelm Miller, "Successful American Gardens VIII," *Country Life in America* 20, no. 9 (1 September 1911): 35–38.

24. Ibid., 38.

25. The increasing popularity of gardens and Miller's articles led Doubleday, Page and Co. to select him as the founding editor of *The Garden Magazine* in 1905. In contrast to his tastemaking, inspirational *Country Life* articles, Miller's *Garden* essays were more technical.

26. Although he no longer edited *Country Life in America* and *The Garden Magazine*, Miller continued to write for the magazines after he moved to Illinois.

27. Wilhelm Miller, "How the Middle West Can Come into Its Own," *Country Life in America* 22, no. 10 (15 September 1912): 11.

28. Thomas E. Tallmadge, "The 'Chicago School,'" *Architectural Review* 15, no. 4 (April 1908): 69–74. Tallmadge himself was a member.

29. The actual date of Jensen's design is uncertain. Jensen recollected the date as 1888, less than two years after he began employment with the park district as a laborer. Grese suggested that the garden may have been designed as late as 1894. See Jens Jensen, "Natural Parks and Gardens," *Saturday Evening Post* 202, no. 36 (8 March 1930): 19, and Grese, *Jens Jensen*, 7–8.

30. James [Jens] Jensen, "The Symmetrical and the Natural Flower Garden," *Park and Cemetery* 10, no. 7 (September 1900): 160.

31. *The Sketchbook: A Magazine Devoted to the Fine Arts* 6, no. 1 (September 1906): 21–28.

32. Miller's 1901 date for the Rubens project is incorrect; Jensen's earliest drawings for the project are dated 1903. Jensen's planting plan for the Rubens pool is reproduced in Grese, *Jens Jensen*, 97. Jensen revised the garden for its later owner, James Simpson, in 1913.

33. Jens Jensen, *Siftings* (Chicago: Ralph Fletcher Seymour, 1939), 34.

34. George W. Maher, "The Western Spirit," *Western Architect* 9, no. 12 (December 1906): 125. Maher originally delivered the text in a March 1906 lecture to the Chicago Architectural Club. As Jensen was a member, he may have been in Maher's audience.

35. Jens Jensen, "Beauty and Fitness in Park Concrete Work," *Park and Cemetery* 18, no. 9 (November 1908): 435–36.

36. See illustrations in Jens Jensen, "An Open-air Exhibition of American Sculpture," *Architectural Review* 16, no. 5 (May 1909): 57–59.

37. Frank A. Waugh, *The Landscape Beautiful: A Study of the Utility of the Natural Landscape, Its Relation to Human Life and Happiness, with the Application of These Principles in Landscape Gardening, and in Art in General* (New York: Orange Judd, 1910). Like Miller, Waugh published in *Country Life in America* and *The Garden Magazine* and was an associate of Bailey. Also see Linda Flint McClelland's entry on Waugh in Birnbaum and Karson, *Pioneers*, 434–36.

38. Ibid., 174. Waugh qualified that Jensen's designs resembled "the more modern work in Germany." It is unclear whether Waugh actually saw Jensen's work.

39. Waugh, *The Landscape*, 199.

40. Miller may have had a limited familiarity with Jensen's work prior to Waugh's book. In a 1908 unsigned editorial, Miller reported that "in the West Side parks system of Chicago, concrete has been used very effectively in making garden benches by Mr. Jens Jensen." See "Editorial Note," *Garden Magazine* 7, no. 5 (June 1908): 278.

41. "Let Nature Be Your Teacher," *Construction News* 33, no. 16 (20 April 1912): 8–9.

42. Jensen had "an intimate acquaintance with the best European models." Waugh, *Landscape*, 174. As well, Jensen was not oblivious to American precedent. See Grese, *Jens Jensen*, 10–61.

43. See, for example, Jensen's "Soil Conditions and Tree Growth around Lake Michigan," *Park and Cemetery* 14, nos. 2, 3 (April, May 1904): 24–25, 42. Although Jensen published earlier botanical studies, they focused upon individual plant species and varieties, not relations with soil type and landform.

44. The author thanks Paul Kruty for consulting *The Lakeside Annual Directory of the City of Chicago* (Chicago: Chicago Directory, 1908) on his behalf.

45. Jensen's work was included in the 1905 and 1907 annual exhibitions of the Chicago Architectural Club in the Art Institute of Chicago. See *Eighteenth Annual Exhibition of the Chicago Architectural Club in the Galleries of the Art Institute* (Chicago: n.p., 1905) and *Catalogue of the Twentieth Annual Exhibition of the Chicago Architectural Club* (Chicago: n.p., 1907). On the club and its activities, see Brooks, *The Prairie School*, 27–44.

46. Many, but not all, of the architects with whom Jensen worked are listed in Grese's "Appendix A: Jensen's Projects," *Jens Jensen*, 199–220.

47. Wright informed Miller that "the first important work which recognized artistically the influence of the prairie, so far as I know, was the Winslow House, designed in 1893." Wright, however, did not explain how this influence was expressed in the design. Wright to Miller, 24 February 1915, *Frank Lloyd Wright: Letters to Architects*, ed. Bruce Brooks Pfeiffer (Fresno: Press at California State University, 1984), 49–52.

48. Manson, *Frank Lloyd Wright*, 72. Wright's boulder motif also was indebted to the Boston architect H. H. Richardson's work.

49. Robert C. Spencer Jr., "The Work of Frank Lloyd Wright," *Architectural Review* 7, no. 6 (June 1900): 61. Spencer also included two photographs of Wright's Chauncey Williams house, including a detail view of the boulder-framed doorway.

50. Ibid.

51. Ibid., 62.

52. Jensen later published his own work in *The Architectural Review*. See Jens Jensen, "Some Gardens of the Middle West," 15, no. 5 (May 1908): 93–95, and "An Open-Air Exhibition of American Sculpture," 16, no. 5 (May 1909): 57–59.

53. See Wright's lecture text, "Concerning Landscape Architecture" (1900), in Bruce Brooks Pfeiffer, ed., *Frank Lloyd Wright: Collected Writings, 1894–1930* (New York: Rizzoli, 1992), 54–57.

54. Ibid., 74.

55. Frank Lloyd Wright, "In the Cause of Architecture," *Architectural Record* 23, no. 3 (March 1908): 157.

56. Ibid.

57. Miller met Rogers at Cornell, and they wed 8 June 1899. The Millers had a daughter, Ruth Rogers Miller (Mrs. Leonard R. Thompson) (1903–?) and a son, Farrand Rogers Miller (1909–?). DAF. Mary Farrand Rogers was a naturalist and educator of note. She "served as an instructor in large summer schools held in nature study at Ithaca [and] in 1899 started the Home Nature Study Course leaflets." See Rodgers, *Liberty Hyde Bailey*, 216–17. Rogers also wrote *The Brook Book* (New York: Doubleday, Page, 1902).

58. In testament of Miller's popularity, the editor at *Country Life* reported: "Since the beginning, this magazine has struck the note of authority in at least one thing, and that is horticulture. We venture to say that *Country Life* has done as much as any agency to raise the standard of life in the country, through the inspiration of its horticultural articles. We are happy to say that the success of this most important feature of the magazine is due largely to Dr. Wilhelm Miller. His unflagging enthusiasm has been manifest in these pages since the very beginning, and we are profoundly grateful for his invaluable help. He is without doubt the most profound student of gardening in America." See "An Appreciation and a Greeting," *Country Life in America* 23, no. 2 (December 1912): 17. Miller's advice was featured in advertisements for Highlands Nursery (at Boxford, Massachusetts) in *Park and Cemetery* 23, no. 3 (May 1913): 8. His book *What England Can Teach Us about Gardening* was released in a second edition in 1913.

59. Review of *What England Can Teach Us about Gardening*, by Wilhelm Miller, *Landscape Architecture Quarterly* 2, no. 2 (January 1912): 99.

60. E[dmund]. [Jane] James to Wilhelm Miller, 21 October 1912, SF. Miller was appointed for "three years from September 1, 1912." Miller later reported that he had "become the last thing in the world [he] expected to be[:] a lecturer" and that he liked his "new tool, the lantern slide as well as the pen." See Wilhelm Miller, "'Landscape Extension' in the Middle West," *Garden Magazine* 21, no. 1 (February 1915): 42.

61. Charles Mulford Robinson, "City Planning Course at the University of Illinois," *Landscape Architecture Quarterly* 3, no. 3 (April 1913): 98. Robinson's city planning position was the first in the nation. See Amy Brown's entry on Robinson in Birnbaum and Karson, *Pioneers*, 315–18.

62. Nicholas Vachel Lindsay, *The Soul of the City Receives the Gift of the Holy Spirit* (Springfield, Ill.: privately published, 1913), n.p. This was a reference to Miller's aim for the "Prairie School of Art."

63. "Is a State Style of Gardening Possible?," *Garden Magazine* 17, no. 6 (July 1913): 336. Miller was the author of this anonymous "News and Comment" feature.

64. Wilhelm Miller, "Landscape Extension," in *The Standard Cyclopedia of Horticulture*, vol. 4, ed. L. H. Bailey (New York: Macmillan, 1916), 1816. Miller explained that the "phrase 'landscape extension' was used officially in February 1914, at the University of Illinois. Prior to that, university extension work in landscape gardening has been undertaken in several states, notably at Massachusetts [by Frank Waugh], but incidentally to regular teaching." The Division of Landscape Extension was distinct from the University's professional Division of Landscape Gardening.

65. By June 1913 Miller had developed seven illustrated lectures: "An American Style of Landscape Gardening," "The 'Illinois Way' of Neighborhood Planting," "The 'Illinois Way' of Landscape Gardening," "The 'Illinois Way' of Beautifying the Farm," "The 'Illinois Way' of Roadside Planting," "The 'Illinois Way' of Street Tree Management," and "New Ways of Creating Popular Interest in Landscape Gardening." Miller to L. H. Bailey, 23 June 1913, Bailey MSS.

66. Miller formulated three criteria for his object-lesson design projects. "1. The project must be educational. Therefore it should not compete with landscape gardeners, and it should be the smallest unit that will stimulate a large amount of designing and planting. 2. It should be for public, not private, benefit. Therefore, front yards may be designed in street plans, but not back yards, except for corner and vacant lots where screening of unsightly objects may be necessary. 3. A reasonable guarantee must be furnished before the plan is made, that a definite sum of money will be spent, if the plans are acceptable, and adequate provision must be made for maintenance." See Wilhelm Miller, "Landscape Extension," in Bailey, *The Standard Cyclopedia of Horticulture*, vol. 4, 1815.

Landscape architects known to have worked for Miller in the Division of Landscape Extension include: Franz August Aust; Herbert Wardwell Blaney (a landscape architecture graduate of Harvard and former employee of Boston landscape architect Warren Manning); Edwin Deal; Lawrence Earl Fogelsong; Leon Deming Titlon; and John Raymond Van Kleek. Records of the Department of Horticulture, University Archives, University of Illinois at Urbana–Champaign (hereafter cited as Horticulture Records).

Documentation of the landscape designs prepared by Miller's staff is fragmentary. Projects for which records survive were all prepared in ca. 1914–15 for rural Illinois towns, Horticulture Records. A selection includes the grounds of the Belleville Savings Bank; Kimmerer Orphans Home at Assumption; the Mattson Public Library at Princeton; the post office at Decatur; the design for Leaverton Park at Palestine; and farmstead plans for W. F. Barton at Homer, A. S. Postlewait at Palestine, and H. J. Sconce at Sidell. Sconce was a noted Illinois agriculturalist and also wrote about Miller's work for him. See H. J. Sconce, *The Romance of Everifarm*

(New York: Macmillan, 1922). Other projects also were published in Miller's experiment station circulars. See Wilhelm Miller, "The First Roadside Planting along the Lincoln Highway," *American City* 14, no. 4 (April 1916): 325–29. Also of note is "Design for Arrangement and Planting of a Small Park and Town Approach at Sycamore, Ill.," color rendering dated May 1915. Franz A. Aust Papers, State Historical Society of Wisconsin, Madison (hereafter cited as Aust MSS).

67. Wilhelm Miller, *The "Illinois Way" of Beautifying the Farm*, University of Illinois Agricultural Experiment Station Circular no. 170 (Urbana, 1914). From its inception in 1888, the University of Illinois station published circulars to disseminate experiment results and practical advice to rural Illinois. Miller described these circulars as "practical" and "essential." For the purposes of his landscape extension activities, however, Miller advocated a modified format, as the traditional circular "presupposed general interest in [ornamental] planting." Instead, Miller preferred an "inspirational" circular, a "publication that contains many illustrations, for the reason that landscape gardening is not exact but comparative, the pictures may well be arranged in contrasting pairs." See Wilhelm Miller, "Landscape Extension," Bailey, *The Standard Cyclopedia of Horticulture*, vol. 4, 1813–16.

68. Miller, *The "Illinois Way*," 2–3.

69. Miller was likely aware of Robert Spencer's work before coming to Illinois. Of all the Chicago architects, Spencer no doubt had the greatest affinity for the agricultural nature of Miller's work. In 1900–1, for instance, Spencer designed seven farmhouse prototypes for *The Ladies' Home Journal*. He also published his work in *Country Life in America* during Miller's horticultural editorship. See Robert C. Spencer Jr., "Attractive Farmhouses for Real Farmers," *Country Life in America* 6, no. 6 (October 1904): 546–48. See Brooks, *The Prairie School*, 57–61.

70. Miller, *The "Illinois Way*," 3–4. Miller also included sculptor Lorado Taft, author Hamlin Garland, poet Vachel Lindsay, and painters Frank C. Peyraud and Charles Francis Browne as members of the "Prairie School of Art."

71. Ibid., 1.

72. Although today suggestive of a racist sensibility, Miller's terminology actually reflects his (and Jensen's) synthesis of "progressive, democratic ideals with the theory of environmental determinism" of the day. See Dave Egan and William H. Tishler, "Jens Jensen, Native Plants, and the Concept of Nordic Superiority," *Landscape Journal* 18, no. 1 (Spring 1999): 11–29.

73. For Cowles, his role in the development of plant ecology, and his relationship with Jensen and Miller, see J. Ronald Engel, *Sacred Sands: The Struggle for Community in the Indiana Dunes* (Middletown, Conn.: Wesleyan University Press, 1983). Also see Grese, *Jens Jensen*, 120–36.

74. This approach has marked affinities with a technique developed earlier by German landscape architect Willy Lange. Frank Waugh studied with Lange in Germany and in 1910 reported to Americans that Lange's novel approach was named "the biological-physiognomical" or "ecological method." Waugh explained that Lange's "theory asserts that plants should be assembled in a garden in their natural relationships—placing together those plants which associate with one another in nature, placing such plant society in its proper soil and on its proper geologic formation." See F. A. Waugh, "German Landscape Gardening," *Country Gentleman* 75, no. 3004 (25 August 1910): 790. Jensen and Miller were likely aware of Lange's efforts through Waugh. Waugh's report appeared the same year that he promoted Jensen's work in *The Landscape Beautiful* (see note 37). Later, Miller also published in *The Country Gentleman*. See, for example, his "Shrubs for a Small Lot," 79, no. 41 (10 October 1914): 32. On Jensen and German garden design, see Christopher Vernon, "Frank Lloyd Wright, Walter Burley Griffin, Jens Jensen, and the Jugendstil Garden in America," *Die Gartenkunst* 7, no. 2 (1995): 232–46.

75. Of the thirty-five illustrations of work by landscape architects in Miller's circular, twenty-four were by Jensen, ten by Simonds, and one by Warren H. Manning. Moreover, Jensen is quoted by name throughout the text. In some places, however, Miller quotes Jensen anonymously, referring to him as "one of the older men" (3), "one of the progressive or prairie group" (4), "the designer" (14), "one park designer" (15), "one Illinois landscape gardener" (18), and "a resident of Ravinia, Illinois" (20). Concealing Jensen's identity countered concern that he was "advertising" Jensen alone and implicitly furthered his premise that Prairie School membership was more extensive than the designers mentioned by name. Within the context of Miller's promotion of a school versus an individual, see Wright's comments to Miller, note 88.

76. Simonds to Miller, 20 July 1915, Horticulture Records. Simonds also did not share Miller's (and Jensen's) view that Jensen's Humboldt Park

conservatory gardens were "a free restoration of ancient Illinois" (see *The Prairie Spirit*, 8–9). For Simonds, this connection "with the prairie is rather far fetched." Simonds eventually mused, "As I read your manuscript, I sometimes wonder if you do not try to make facts fit a theory rather than theory fit facts."

77. Lathrop to Miller, 27 April 1915, Horticulture Records. Lathrop was educated in Europe and a commissioner of Chicago's Lincoln Park. Miller reported that Lathrop "discovered" Simonds, then an architect and engineer, and "persuaded him to become a landscape gardener." See Miller, *The Prairie Spirit*, 2.

78. Julia Sniderman Bachrach, "Ossian Cole Simonds: Conservation Ethic in the Prairie Style," in Tishler, *Midwestern Landscape Architecture*, 95.

79. Once in Australia, however, Griffin soon championed the use of native flora in landscape design, largely owing to its sculptural qualities. On Griffin as a landscape architect, see Christopher Vernon, "'Expressing Natural Conditions with Maximum Possibility': The American Landscape Art of Walter Burley Griffin," *Journal of Garden History* 15, no. 1 (Spring 1995): 19–47, and "The Landscape Art of Walter Burley Griffin," in *Beyond Architecture: Marion Mahony and Walter Burley Griffin, America, Australia, India*, ed. Anne Watson (Sydney: Powerhouse [Museum] Publishing, 1998), 86–103.

80. Miller to Griffin, 5 February 1914, Horticulture Records.

81. *Transactions of the American Society of Landscape Architects: 1909–1921*, ed. and comp. Carl Rust Parker, Bremer W. Pond, and Theodora Kimball (Boston: ASLA, 1922), 28.

82. On Manning and his own nationalist agenda, including discussion of Miller, see Robin Karson's excellent study, "Warren H. Manning: Pragmatist in the Wild Garden," in *Nature and Ideology: Natural Garden Design in the Twentieth Century*, ed. Joachim Wolschke-Bulmahn (Washington, D.C.: Dumbarton Oaks Research Library and Collection, 1997), 113–30, and her entry on Manning in Birnbaum and Karson, *Pioneers*, 236–42. Also see Virginia Tuttle Clayton, "Wild Gardening and the Popular American Magazine, 1890–1918," in Wolschke-Bulmahn, *Nature and Ideology*, 131–54.

83. *Transactions*, 28. Simonds was then president of the ASLA. At the meeting, Miller "discussed University Extension Work in the general field of landscape gardening."

84. Nancy Price, "Walter Burley Griffin," B. Arch. thesis, University of Sydney, 1933. This document was prepared in consultation with Griffin. As Simonds also knew, opportunities to practice of landscape architecture in Chicago then were not promising. In 1902, for example, only six "landscape gardeners" (and no "landscape architects") were included in *The Lakeside Annual Directory of the City of Chicago* (Chicago: Chicago Directory, 1902), 2436–37. Even as late as 1912, only two landscape architects and thirteen landscape gardeners were listed. Ibid. (1912), 1552 and 1693.

85. Both Jensen and Griffin displayed their work in the club's 1905 and 1907 annual exhibitions; see note 45.

86. Jensen explained that "masters like Louis Sullivan, Frank L. Wright, Walter Griffin, [and poets] Vachel Lindsay and Carl Sandburg are all of mid-American growth." See Jens Jensen, "Landscape Appreciation," *Wisconsin Horticulture* 17, no. 9 (May 1927): 129–30 and 146–47.

87. Simonds to Miller, 20 July 1915, Horticulture Records. Miller's view is recorded by his annotations to Simonds' letter reviewing *The Prairie Spirit* manuscript. Simonds assessed one of the illustrations, a photograph of Jensen's "prairie river" at Humboldt Park, as "very satisfying" (see *The Prairie Spirit*, fig. 2). In reaction, Miller annotated the passage "generous praise to a rival." Jensen himself also may have seen Simonds in this way. Elsewhere in his review, Simonds disagreed with Miller's diagnosis that "storm sewers" were responsible for drying out many of the ravines along Chicago's increasingly suburban North Shore. As Jensen was Miller's source, Miller conveyed Simonds' divergent opinion to Jensen. Jensen defended his position and somewhat antagonistically replied, "I have tramped in those ravines a great deal more than Simonds. Simonds is not known as a tramper or a hiker and I never knew him to spend his life in that way." See Jensen to Miller, 26 July 1915, Horticulture Records. Also indicative of his regard for Simonds' work, Jensen later complained to Waugh that Miller tried—in *The Prairie Spirit*—"to give Simonds and Manning credit for restoration work." In Jensen's view, "they never did any, at least not here [Illinois]." He elaborated that "there is quite a difference in restoring a bluff or a piece of landscape with a lot of plants scattered over America, or restoring the characteristics of the native landscape wherever found." "The first," Jensen concluded, "is the lie and the other is truth—and truth is art." Jens Jensen to Frank Waugh, 13 January 1916, Horticulture Records.

88. Wright to Miller, 24 February 1915, *Frank Lloyd Wright: Letters*, 49–52. Miller's initial letter of queries, to which Wright's is a reply, apparently has not survived. Wright enlarged that "I cannot see how [Sullivan] could figure in any form other than grotesque as the founder of a 'Prairie School of Architecture.'" That Wright used the term in quotation marks strongly suggests Miller's authorship of it. Wright also clarified that "I have acknowledged the influence of the prairie in developing the forms I have used and dedicated types to the prairie, but I have never used the phrase 'Prairie Style of Architecture.'" Again, Wright's use of quotation marks suggests that Miller coined this term.

The architect closed the letter, "I am sorry that an *American* university should feel that the work of a man is only worthy of university recognition and support when it has got far enough along to be recognized as the work of many, loses its individual distinction and becomes a matter of 'the group.'" This passage is significant in that it suggests that Miller's motivation for promoting a 'school' versus an individual may have been imposed by the university.

89. See Wilhelm Miller, "Landscape Extension," in Bailey, *The Standard Cyclopedia of Horticulture*, vol. 4, 1814.

90. The correspondence includes Jensen to Waugh, 21 January 1916; Jensen to Miller, 21 January 1916; Waugh to Jensen, 24 January 1916; Jensen to Miller, 27 January 1916; and Jensen to Waugh, 28 January 1916, Horticulture Records.

91. Waugh's visiting professorship at Illinois in December 1915 was orchestrated largely by Miller. See "Exchange Professorship in Landscape Gardening," *Park and Cemetery* 25, no. 10 (December 1915): 309. Waugh's daughter Dorothy offered insight into Waugh and Miller's friendship, recollecting: "I see Professor Miller [as] animated in movement and speech, eagerly talking with Dad as if there were too little time to begin to explore all they wished to say to one another." Dorothy Waugh to Christopher Vernon, 3 December 1987 (author's possession).

92. Frank Waugh, *The Natural Style in Landscape Gardening* (Boston: Richard G. Badger, 1917).

93. See, for example, James R. Shortridge, *The Middle West: Its Meaning in American Culture* (Lawrence: University Press of Kansas, 1989).

94. See Jefferson's "Plan for the Government of the Western Territory [1784]," in *The Papers of Thomas Jefferson*, vol. 6, ed. Julian P. Boyd (Princeton: Princeton University Press, 1952), 581–600, and "The Northwest Territory [1790]," in ibid., vol. 18 (1971), 159–78. The author thanks C. Allan Brown for these citations.

95. Richard Guy Wilson, "Chicago and the International Arts and Crafts Movements: Progressive and Conservative Tendencies," in *Chicago Architecture 1872–1922: Birth of a Metropolis*, ed. John Zukowsky (Munich: Prestel-Verlag/Art Institute of Chicago, 1987), 217.

96. Irving K. Pond, *The Meaning of Architecture: An Essay in Constructive Criticism* (Boston: Marshall Jones, 1918), 174–75.

97. Miller, *The "Illinois Way,"* 33.

98. Ibid.

99. Jensen shared Miller's concern for the authentic. See, for example, his reaction to Simonds's and Manning's work as "restoration," note 87.

100. Review of *The Prairie Spirit in Landscape Gardening*, by Wilhelm Miller, *Landscape Architecture Quarterly* 6 (1916): 163–64.

101. Miller to Jensen, 5 May 1916, Horticulture Records.

102. Peter B. Wight, "Country House Architecture in the Middle West," *Architectural Record* 40, no. 4 (October 1916): 590–92.

103. Ibid.

104. McFarland to Dr. Joseph C. Blair, 10 January 1916, Horticulture Records. Blair then was head of the Department of Horticulture. Also see E. Lynn Miller's entry on McFarland in Birnbaum and Karson, *Pioneers*, 249–51.

105. Blair to McFarland, 6 January 1916, Horticulture Records. Miller's reputation for his "inspirational" articles was well-established prior to his joining the Illinois faculty. Paradoxically, it was this quality of Miller's work that seems to have been the source of Blair's dissatisfaction. Given this, and the fact that Blair was Miller's former classmate at Cornell, one wonders as to the dynamics of the relationship between Miller and Blair.

106. Karl B. Lohmann, "An Opinion on Landscape Extension," *Landscape Architecture Quarterly* 12, no. 2 (January 1922): 89. Lohmann was then head of the University of Illinois' Division of Landscape Gardening.

107. Eugene Davenport to Joseph Blair, 2 July 1915, Horticulture Records. Dean Davenport decided to extend Miller's contract by one year "with the understanding that . . . [Miller] should feel free to accept any other more favorable engagement at any time in the interim."

108. Aust took up an appointment as Associate Professor of Landscape Design in the University of Wisconsin's Department of Horticulture in 1915. Through Miller, Aust developed friendships with Jensen and Wright.

For Aust's activities at Madison, see his "The State Program—Wisconsin," *Landscape Architecture Quarterly* 12, no. 2 (January 1922): 69–73. Aust awaits a biographer.

109. Wilhelm Miller, "The Minnesota Spirit in Landscape Gardening," *Minnesotan: The Individual, the Home, the Community* 1, no. 7 (February 1916): 7–13.

110. In the manuscript version of his "The Minnesota Spirit in Landscape Gardening," Miller listed "Purcell and Elmslie of Minneapolis [et. al.]" as among the membership of the "Middle Western school" who were "willing to accept the name prairie style," Horticulture Records. Elmslie ran the partnership's office in Chicago. No mention of Purcell and Elmslie was made in *The Prairie Spirit*. This passage was omitted from the version published in *The Minnesotan*.

111. Miller to Lindsay, 14 March 1916, Horticulture Records. Miller also requested that Lindsay send a copy of the latter's poem "The Lotus and the Rose" to Wright. On Wright's movements and work of this period, see Anthony Alofsin's outstanding *Frank Lloyd Wright: The Lost Years, 1910–1922* (Chicago: University of Chicago Press, 1993).

112. The 11 January 1917 *Cornell Alumni News* reported that "Wilhelm Miller announces that he has opened an office for the practice of landscape architecture, at 700 Steinway Hall, 64 East Van Buren Street, Chicago" (165). Actually, this decision may have marked Miller's realization of an earlier plan. Rogers reported that the University of Illinois offer preempted Miller's plan to study landscape architecture at "the Bussey Institution in Boston." See Rogers, *[Wilhelm Miller:] His Life Story*. Miller also contemplated returning east "to practice landscape architecture at Philadelphia." Wilhelm Miller to E. E. Kendall, 24 April 1916, Horticulture Records.

Miller's first article published under the title "Landscape Architect" was "Foundation Planting," *Garden Magazine* 24, no. 3 (October 1916): 86–88. His Chicago address is also confirmed in "Collaborators," in Bailey, *The Standard Cyclopedia of Horticulture*, vol. 6, 3558. Also in 1917, Miller again published under the byline "Landscape Architect, Chicago, Illinois." See his "The Use of the Rose in the Landscape" in *The American Rose Annual: The 1917 Year-book of Rose Progress*, vol. 2, ed. J. Horace McFarland (Harrisburg, Penn.: American Rose Society, 1918), 12–15.

113. Jensen's practice remained at Steinway Hall until 1918. See Grese, *Jens Jensen*, 137. Given their friendship, Jensen's presence likely influenced Miller's choice of location. Alternatively, might competition for clientele also have been an unanticipated outcome of their mutual pursuit of landscape architecture (even within the same building)?

114. Wilhelm Miller, "The Prairie Style of Landscape Architecture," *Architectural Record* 40, no. 6 (December 1916): 590–92.

115. William Gray Purcell to Mark L. Peisch ("Memo—Wilhelm Miller"), undated (ca. 1950s), Mark L. Peisch Papers, Avery Architectural and Fine Arts Library, Columbia University. Purcell remembered that "Of course P[urcell] & E[lmslie] knew him [Miller]—who did not among the living. George [Elmslie] knew him personally, as George was in the Chicago office most of the time after 1912. . . . [Work] For us—I'm not sure—records gone. Perhaps Hunter, Flossmoor?" The author thanks Paul Kruty for calling this document to his attention. George Elmslie himself earlier reported that he "had a very pleasant discussion with Professor Miller who is no longer a professor but a landscape gardener, now in Chicago, also in good standing." George Grant Elmslie to Annette Kellerman, "about Oct. 1916" (annotation by Purcell), William Gray Purcell Papers, Northwest Architectural Archives, Minneapolis (hereafter cited as Purcell MSS). Also see Mark Hammons's superb "Purcell and Elmslie, Architects," in *Minnesota 1900: Art and Life on the Upper Mississippi, 1890–1915*, ed. Michael Conforti (Newark: University of Delaware Press, 1994), 214–77.

116. Even as late as 1919, Miller remained interested in collaborating with Purcell, directly stating that he "would like very well to design the landscape" for one of Purcell's houses. Miller "was confident that [he] could do it better than an eastern man, because [he] understand[s] the spirit of your architecture, and [believed that] eastern [landscape] architects do not." Miller to Purcell, 14 October 1919, Purcell MSS.

117. Wilhelm Miller, "'Ragtime' Gardening—and Something Better," *Minnesotan* 2, no. 9 (March 1917): 28–29.

118. In addition to the articles cited in note 112, see Wilhelm Miller, "Planting for Privacy of the Home," *Garden Magazine* 25, no. 3 (April 1917): 169–70.

119. Thomas E. Tallmadge, "The Thirtieth Annual Architectural Exhibit in Chicago," *Western Architect* 25 (April 1917): 27–28.

120. David Van Zanten, *Sullivan's City: The Meaning of Ornament for Louis Sullivan* (New York: Norton, 2000), 94. Van Zanten elaborates that "Griffin and Mahony went to Australia in 1913 [actually 1914]; Wright—

tainted by marital troubles in 1909—was devastated by the Taliesin tragedy of 1914 and retreated to Japan and Los Angeles, Sullivan's 1913 display at the Chicago Architectural Club exhibition was his swansong and only a retrospective."

121. Miller, along with his wife, appears in the 1916–17 and 1919–20 membership directories of Detroit's Society of Arts and Crafts (in the latter as "William Tyler Miller"). See the *Eleventh* and *Thirteenth Annual Report of the Society of Arts and Crafts, Detroit, Michigan* (Detroit: Society of Arts and Crafts, 1918, 1920), 38, 35 respectively. In 1920 Miller reported that he was a "Landscape Architect" in Detroit from 1916 to 1920. His omission of Chicago suggests that his practice there was short-lived, perhaps only months in duration. "Record for General Catalogue of Alumni and Former Students," University of Michigan Archives, Ann Arbor. The author thanks Barbara Geiger for calling this source to his attention.

122. "Dr. Frederick A. Davis—Madison, Wisconsin—Planting Plan for Home Grounds—Wilhelm Miller, Landscape Architect, Detroit, Michigan, October, 1917," Aust MSS. The drawing also bears the monograms "C.T." (Charles Tirrell) and "H.A.L." and the notation "Revised 11.1.17." A separate "Planting List—Flowers, Ferns, Etc.," signed "Wilhelm Miller, Landscape Architect" and dated 12 August 1918, also accompanies the drawing. Tirrell's monogram also appears on this list. That Miller's drawing is included among Aust's papers raises the possibility that Aust may have been involved with the commission.

The Davis property is situated within the precincts of a suburban community, the Highlands, designed by O. C. Simonds in 1911. Miller's client was a world-renowned eye surgeon, according to Rishord. Davis's house, Edenfred, and its site were of note. Designed by H. H. Waterman, the house is "situated at the crest of a hill" and "commands a twenty-mile vista stretching to the far shores of Lake Mendota." See Norman K. Rishord, *Madison's Highlands, a Community with a Land Ethic* (Madison: Highlands Association, 1988), 16. The author thanks William H. Tishler for calling this source to his attention and for Tishler's research in Madison on his behalf.

123. Charles Almon Tirrell was graduated from Massachusetts in 1906. By 1913 he had moved to Chicago and was working for Jensen. The exact date that Tirrell's partnership with Miller began is unclear. Tirrell is listed in the 1916 *Lakeside Annual Directory of the City of Chicago* as a "civil engineer" at "815, 64 E Van Buren," Jensen's Steinway Hall office address. Tirrell is not listed in the 1917 directory. That Tirrell's "C.T." monogram appears on Miller's October 1917 planting plan for Frederick Davis (see previous note) suggests that Tirrell came to Detroit with Miller in 1917. Partnership, then, likely was a later promotion. The author thanks Jack Ahern, Department of Landscape Architecture and Regional Planning, and Michael Milewski, Special Collections and Archives, at University of Massachusetts Amherst for consulting Tirrell's alumnae files on his behalf.

Architect Taylor Woolley (1884–1965), a former apprentice of Wright, knew Tirrell when the latter was still in Jensen's employ. Woolley explained that Tirrell "was one of Jens Jenson's [*sic*] head men. I had him on [the Henry] Ford residence. Later had partnership with Wm. Miller—author of *What England Can Teach About Gardening*. Miller and Terrell [*sic*]." This passage is marginalia in Woolley's own copy of *City Residential Land Development: Studies in Planning: Competitive Plans for Subdividing a Typical Quarter Section of Land in the Outskirts of Chicago*, ed. Alfred B. Yeomans (Chicago: University of Chicago Press, 1916), 87. This page analyzes a plan by Tirrell. The author is grateful to Woolley's biographer, Peter L. Goss, for alerting him to this source and supplying a copy of same. A 1915 letter on Jensen's office letterhead confirms that Tirrell was then in Jensen's employ and at work on Henry Ford's estate, Fairlane. Charles A. Tirrell to Mrs. Henry Ford, 12 April 1915. Fairlane Papers, Henry Ford Museum and Greenfield Village Research Center, Dearborn, Michigan.

124. The name of the practice is confirmed by two letters, Miller to William Gray Purcell, 3 September 1919 and 14 October 1919, Purcell MSS. "Miller and Tirrell, Landscape Architects" letterhead lists "William Tyler Miller" and "Charles A. Tirrell" at "715–719 Stevens Building, Detroit." These letters are also important as they contain references to two other Miller and Tirrell commissions. In the former letter Miller refers to his and Tirrell's design for "a bunch of lots" on Detroit's Boston Boulevard for a Phillip H. Gray. In the latter, Miller alludes to a "kind of democratized outdoor theatre or player's green on the scale of a city lot, which my partner and I are designing." The label "player's green" was earlier coined by Jensen to describe his own theater designs.

125. Harlow O. Whittemore [1889–1986] to Mara Gelbloom, undated [ca. 1974], Harlow Olin Whittemore Papers, Michigan Historical Collections, Bentley Historical Library, University of Michigan (hereafter cited as Whittemore MSS).

126. C. Harold Wills (1878–1940), a former associate of Henry Ford,

earlier had commissioned Frank Lloyd Wright to design his house. When Wright decided to travel to Europe, the commission fell to his successor Marion Mahony, who later married Walter Burley Griffin. See Brooks, *The Prairie School*, 149–53.

On Marysville, see, for example, the promotional leaflet *C. Harold Wills: He Built a City to Build a Motor Car* (Marysville, Mich.: C. H. Wills and Co. Motor Cars, 1921), National Automotive History Collection, Detroit Public Library. Although unsigned, the plan of Marysville is included in another promotional leaflet, *Marysville: The Proof of Ten Months' Progress*, 15 September 1920, C. Harold Wills Papers, Henry Ford Museum and Greenfield Village Research Center (hereafter cited as Wills MSS). This document reported that the construction of Marysville began on 15 November 1919.

127. "Landscape Man at Marysville," *Port Huron Herald*, 20 June 1919, Wills scrapbooks, Wills MSS.

128. Whittemore to Mara Gelbloom, undated [ca. 1974], Whittemore MSS. Ultimately, Whittemore classified "Miller as a horticultural writer and lecturer rather than a designer."

129. Transcript of "Interview with Alfred Caldwell conducted by Robert Grese and Julia Sniderman, 31 January 1987," 3 (copy in author's possession). The late Alfred Caldwell (1903–1998) also was a landscape architect who worked for Jensen. Caldwell's cousin was married to Tirrell. At this author's request, Grese queried Caldwell for knowledge of Miller. According to Caldwell, Tirrell's partnership with Miller "didn't work" as "Charlie didn't like him as a partner. He thought he [Miller] was terribly effeminate and he made Charlie very uneasy." On Caldwell and his relationship with "Terrel [sic]," see *Alfred Caldwell: The Life and Work of a Prairie School Landscape Architect*, ed. Dennis Domer (Baltimore: Johns Hopkins University Press, 1997), 3–6 and 283 n. 13. Also see Domer's entry on Caldwell in Birnbaum and Karson, *Pioneers*, 43–47.

130. William Tyler Miller, "Shrubs and Vines for California Gardens," *Garden Magazine* 32, no. 4 (December 1920): 191–93. Confirming the long absence of Miller's contributions, the editor prefaced: "The author of this article who will be remembered by many old readers as the first editor of *The Garden Magazine*, is now resident of California."

131. Rogers, *[Wilhelm Miller:] His Life Story*. This author has been unable to document the details of Rogers's mention of "extension work in the University of California." In 1925 and 1930, Miller reported his occupation as "writer, editor, teacher, and fruit-grower," in *R[ural] U[plook] S[ervice]: A Preliminary Attempt to Register the Rural Leadership in the United States and Canada*, ed. L. H. Bailey (Ithaca, 1925, 1930), 472, 482. Like Wilhelm's wife Mary, her sister Julia Ellen Rogers was a Cornell naturalist of note.

132. See Miller to "Frank Lloyd Wright c/o Jens Jensen," 28 March 1934, Frank Lloyd Wright Archives, Taliesin, Scottsdale, Arizona. The author thanks Bruce Brooks Pfeiffer for providing him with a copy of this letter. Miller to "Brudder Jens [Jensen]," 17 December 1937; and Miller to Jensen, 11 January 1938 [Miller died that March], Morton Arboretum, Lisle, Illinois. The author thanks Patricia Takemoto for calling the Jensen letters to his attention.

133. Thomas E. Tallmadge, "Country House Architecture in the Middle West," *Architectural Record* 53, no. 4 (October 1922): 285–97.

134. Ibid., 292.

135. Ibid., 294–96.

136. Jens Jensen, "Natural Parks and Gardens," *Saturday Evening Post* 202, no. 36 (8 March 1930): 19.

A Selected Bibliography of Wilhelm Tyler Miller's Published Works

CHRISTOPHER VERNON

The chronological order of this bibliography enables one to trace the evolution of Miller's interests—from the single plant to the broadest of landscape designs. Miller's output reached its apogee in the 1909–12 period. His 1908 study trip to England was the catalyst for an outburst of publications that began this period, resulting in a parallel series of articles in *Country Life in America* and *The Garden Magazine*. Miller later collated and revised these, including them in his book *What England Can Teach Us about Gardening*. After he began work at the University of Illinois in 1912, his time available for writing diminished.

Even at 144 citations, this bibliography is necessarily incomplete. Miller is known to have published under (as yet unidentified) pen names, and many of the unsigned editorials in *Country Life* and *Garden* were doubtless authored by him. Miller also contributed numerous entries to Bailey's *Cyclopedia of American Horticulture* and its successor, *The Standard Cyclopedia of Horticulture*, in addition to the sources cited below.

Unless otherwise cited, all publications are attributed to Miller as "Wilhelm Miller."

CL   *Country Life in America*
GF   *Garden and Forest*
GM   *The Garden Magazine*

"Chrysanthemums at Cornell University." *GF* 8, no. 404 (20 November 1895): 466.

L. H. Bailey, Wilhelm Miller, and C. E. Hunn. *The 1895 Chrysanthemums*. Cornell University Agricultural Experiment Station Bulletin no. 112 (Ithaca, N.Y., February 1896).

"Begonia Socotrana." *GF* 9, no. 419 (4 March 1896): 96.

"Chrysanthemums and Dahlias." A.M. thesis, Cornell University, 1897.

A Talk about Dalhias. Cornell University Agricultural Experiment Station Bulletin no. 128 (Ithaca, N.Y., February 1897).

L. H. Bailey and Wilhelm Miller. *Chrysanthemums of 1896*. Cornell University Agricultural Experiment Station Bulletin no. 136 (Ithaca, N.Y., May 1897).

"Garden Annuals from the Plant Breeder's Standpoint." *GF* 10, no. 505 (27 October 1897): 425–26.

"Chrysanthemum Novelties of 1897." *GF* 10, no. 508 (17 November 1897): 454.

"Recent Importations among Chrysanthemums." *GF* 10, no. 509 (24 November 1897): 465.

"The Pink Color in Chrysanthemums." *GF* 10, no. 511 (8 December 1897): 487.

Fourth Report upon Chrysanthemums. Cornell University Agricultural Experiment Station Bulletin no. 147 (Ithaca, N.Y., April 1898).

"Chrysanthemums." Ph.D. diss., Cornell University, 1900.

L. H. Bailey, ed., and Wilhelm Miller, assoc. ed. *Cyclopedia of American Horticulture: Comprising Suggestions for Cultivation of Horticultural Plants, Descriptions of the Species of Fruits, Vegetables, Flowers and Ornamental Plants Sold in the United States and Canada, Together with Geographical and Biographical Sketches*. New York: Macmillan, 1900.

"Wyndhurst: A Summer Home at Lenox." *CL* 2, no. 3 (July 1902): 102–5.

W. M. "Seasonable Suggestions." *CL* 2, no. 5 (September 1902): 191–92.

[W.] M. "Pergolas: A Suggestion." In *How to Make a Flower Garden: A Manual of Practical Information and Suggestions*, edited by Wilhelm Miller, 107–8. New York: Doubleday, Page, 1903.

[W.] M. "Scattered Planting vs. Masses." In *How to Make a Flower Garden: A Manual of Practical Information and Suggestions*, edited by Wilhelm Miller, 52. New York: Doubleday, Page, 1903.

"The Cook Estate at Lenox." *CL* 3, no. 3 (January 1903): 115–17.

"The Sargent Home near Boston." *CL* 3, no. 5 (March 1903): 199–208.

W. M. "An American Idea in Landscape Art." *CL* 4, no. 5 (September 1903): 349–50.

W. M. "Alpine and Iceland Poppies." *GM* 1, no. 2 (March 1905): 75.

"An 'Italian Garden' That Is Full of Flowers." *CL* 7, no. 5 (March 1905): 485–92.

"The Incomparable Japanese Lilies." *GM* 2, no. 4 (November 1905): 174–77.

"Lilies the World Really Needs." *GM* 3, no. 1 (February 1906): 29–30.

"Wild Flowers Worth Cultivating." *CL* 10, no. 3 (July 1906): 322–27.

"The Cultivation of Hardy Orchids." *GM* 4, no. 1 (August 1906): 13–15.

"Summer Window Boxes." *GM* 5, no. 5 (June 1907): 286–88.

"True and False Originality in Garden Design." *GM* 5, no. 6 (July 1907): 334–37, 356.

"Autumn-blooming Crocuses and Their Allies." *GM* 6, no. 2 (September 1907): 135–37.

"Gardens for Special Purposes." *GM* 7, no. 2 (March 1908): 66–69.

"The Best Way to Select Perennial Flowers." *GM* 7, no. 3 (April 1908): 157–60.

"All the Perennial Larkspurs Worth Growing." *GM* 7, no. 4 (May 1908): 214–17.

"Growing Tulips Like Wild Flowers." *CL* 14, no. 5 (September 1908): 450–52, 504–8.

"The Wild and Run-wild Tulips of Europe." *GM* 8, no. 2 (September 1908): 58–61.

"Why Everyone Should Buy Darwin Tulips Now." *GM* 8, no. 3 (October 1908): 130–31.

"The Gorgeous Newly Discovered Tulips." *GM* 8, no. 4 (November 1908): 181–82.

"All the Winter Crocuses Worth Growing." *GM* 8, no. 5 (December 1908): 228–31.

"English Effects with Hardy Conifers." *GM* 8, no. 6 (January 1909): 264–67.

"What England Can Teach Us about Landscape Gardening." *CL* 15, no. 3 (January 1909): 265–68.

"English Effects with Hardy Trees." *GM* 9, no. 1 (February 1909): 23–26.

"What England Can Teach Us about Formal Gardens." *CL* 15, no. 4 (February 1909): 350–53.

"What America Can Teach England about Shrubs." *GM* 9, no. 2 (March 1909): 75–78.

"What England Can Teach Us about Rose Gardens." *CL* 15, no. 5 (March 1909): 467–70.

W. Miller. "English Effects with Broad-leaved Evergreens." *GM* 9, no. 3 (April 1909): 158–62.

"What England Can Teach Us about Making New Varieties." *CL* 15, no. 6 (April 1909): 615–18.

"England's New Kind of Flower Bed." *GM* 9, no. 4 (May 1909): 218–20.

"What England Can Teach Us about Water Gardens." *CL* 16, no. 1 (May 1909): 39–42.

"English Effects with Alpine Flowers." *GM* 9, no. 5 (June 1909): 289–92.

"What England Can Teach Us about Living Outdoors." *CL* 16, no. 2 (June 1909): 175–78.

"How to See English Gardens." *CL* 16, no. 2 (June 1909): 236–40.

"English Effects with Long-lived Bulbs." *GM* 9, no. 6 (July 1909): 343–47.

W. M. "Practical Ideas from England." *GM* 9, no. 6 (July 1909): 360.

"What England Can Teach Us about Wild Gardening." *CL* 16, no. 3 (July 1909): 291–94.

"Why Not Have a Rockery?" *GM* 9, no. 6 (July 1909): 348.

"English Effects with Edging Plants." *GM* 10, no. 1 (August 1909): 18–21.

"What England Can Teach Us about Rock Gardening." *CL* 16, no. 4 (August 1909): 391–94.

"English Effects with Hardy Perennials." *GM* 10, no. 2 (September 1909): 64–67.

"What England Can Teach Us about Hardy Borders." *CL* 16, no. 5 (September 1909): 499–501.

"English Effects with Hardy Climbers." *GM* 10, no. 3 (October 1909): 126–29.

W. M. "Fine Lilies I Saw in England." *GM* 10, no. 3 (October 1909): 142.

"The Right and Wrong Kind of Tropical Effects." *GM* 10, no. 4 (November 1909): 179–82.

"What England Can Teach Us about Wall Gardening." *CL* 17, no. 1 (November 1909): 37–40.

"Lessons from English Cottage Gardens." *GM* 10, no. 5 (December 1909): 227–29.

"What England Can Teach Us about Indoor Gardens." *CL* 17, no. 2 (December 1909): 183–86, 216–18.

"A Famous Avenue of Cedars." *GM* 10, no. 6 (January 1910): 269.

W. M. "American Bog Plants." *GM* 11, no. 1 (February 1910): 32.

"English Effects with Hardy 'Bog Plants.'" *GM* 11, no. 1 (February 1910): 12–14.

"What England Can Teach Us about Peat Gardens." *CL* 17, no. 4 (February 1910): 411–14.

"The Evolution of American Fruit Growing." *GM* 11, nos. 2, 4 (March, May 1910): 76–78, 234–35.

"What England Can Teach Us about Garden Cities." *CL* 17, no. 5 (March 1910): 531–34.

"Gardening Lessons from Bourneville." *CL* 17, no. 5 (March 1910): 618–20.

"The Great Importance of Yew." *GM* 11, no. 3 (April 1910): 170.

"The Right and Wrong Way to Plan a Garden." *GM* 11, no. 6 (July 1910): 346–49.

W. Miller. "The Right and Wrong Kind of 'Show Garden.'" *GM* 12, no. 1 (August 1910): 10–13.

W. M. "A Beautiful Spirea." *GM* 12, no. 2 (September 1910): 88.

W. M. "Practical Ideas from England." *GM* 12, no. 2 (September 1910): 76.

"Practical and Impractical Ideas from England." *GM* 12, nos. 3, 4 (October, November 1910): 114–15, 171–73.

W. M. "A Postscript on Yews." *GM* 12, no. 4 (November 1910): 186.

"Is the Southern Hemlock Better Than the Northern?" *GM* 12, no. 5 (December 1910): 214–15.

The Charm of English Gardens (London: Hodder and Stoughton, 1911).

What England Can Teach Us about Gardening. New York: Doubleday, Page, 1911.

W. M. "About Small Irrigated Farms." *GM* 12, no. 6 (January 1911): 274.

"A Thousand Dollars an Acre from Celery." *GM* 12, no. 6 (January 1911): 262–64.

"The 'Fun' of Collecting Anemones." *GM* 13, nos. 1, 5, 6 (February, June, July 1911): 15–18, 294–96, 354–55.

"Permanent Materials for Your Garden." *GM* 13, no. 3 (April 1911): 154–58.

"Good and Bad Taste in Bedding." *GM* 13, no. 4 (May 1911): 232–34.

"Practical and Impractical Ideas from England." *GM* 13, no. 5 (June 1911): 301.

"The 'Fun' of Collecting Bellflowers." *GM* 14, no. 1 (August 1911): 8–11.

"The 'Fun' of Collecting Hardy Pinks." *GM* 14, no. 2 (September 1911): 54–57.

"Successful American Gardens: VIII. The Higginson Garden." *CL* 20, no. 9 (1 September 1911): 35–38.

"The Umbrella-bearers, a Worthy Family." *GM* 14, no. 4 (November 1911): 169–72.

"Making One Acre Look Like Ten." *GM* 14, no. 5 (December 1911): 206–8.

"The 'Fun' of Collecting Stonecrops." *GM* 14, no. 6, 15, no. 1 (January, February 1912): 254–58, 15–17.

"The Artistic Way of Using Shrubs." *GM* 15, no. 3 (April 1912): 169–70.

"Have We Progressed in Gardening?" *CL* 21, no. 12 (15 April 1912): 26.

"A New Way of Beautifying Large Buildings." *GM* 15, no. 4 (May 1912): 244–46.

"Glimpses of a Brick-walled Garden." *CL* 22, no. 2 (15 May 1912): 19–22.

"Long-lived Evergreens for Gardens." *GM* 15, no. 5 (June 1912): 310–13.

"What Is the Matter with Our Water Gardens?" *CL* 22, no. 4 (15 June 1912): 23–26, 54.

"The Yews in Elizabeth Haddon's Garden." *GM* 15, no. 6 (July 1912): 356–57.

"How to Multiply Your Grounds by Four." *CL* 22, no. 7 (1 August 1912): 34–36.

"Artistic Home Grounds for $300." *GM* 16, no. 2 (September 1912): 50–52.

"The Most Artistic Twenty-acre Place in America." *CL* 22, no. 9 (1 September 1912): 19–22, 50–52.

"How the Middle West Can Come into Its Own." *CL* 22, no. 10 (15 September 1912): 11–14.

"The Principles of Wild Gardening." *GM* 16, no. 3 (October 1912): 105–7.

"The Best Evergreen Vine for America." *GM* 16, no. 4 (November 1912): 155–56.

"Sixty Suggestions for New Gardens." *GM* 16, no. 5 (December 1912): 197–200.

"The Illinois Way of Roadside Planting." In *Fourth Report of the Illinois Highway Commission*, 334–45. Springfield: State of Illinois, 1913.

"Pitch Pine for Poor Soils." *GM* 16, no. 6 (January 1913): 243–44.

W. M. "Turning One's Back on a Vista." *CL* 23, no. 4 (February 1913): 86.

"How to Heighten Western Color." *CL* 23, no. 6 (April 1913): 80–82, 84.

"A New Kind of Western Home." *CL* 23, no. 6 (April 1913): 39–42.

W. M. "Automobiles versus Landscape Gardening." *CL* 24, no. 1 (May 1913): 130.

"The Illinois Way of Roadside Planting." *Illinois Agriculturist* 17, no. 9 (June 1913): 385–89.

[Wilhelm Miller]. "Is a State Style of Gardening Possible?" *GM* 17, no. 6 (July 1913): 336.

"A Refuge from City and Prairie." *GM* 17, no. 6 (July 1913): 337–38.

"Brook Gardens for Every Place and Purse." *CL* 24, no. 4 (August 1913): 40–42.

The "Illinois Way" of Beautifying the Farm. University of Illinois Agricultural Experiment Station Circular no. 170 (Urbana, 1914).

Wilhelm Miller and F. A. Aust. "The Illinois Way of Foundation Planting." In *Illinois Arbor and Bird Days*, 7–19. Springfield: State of Illinois, 1914.

"A Series of Outdoor Salons." *CL* 25, no. 6 (April 1914): 39–40.

"Bird Gardens in the City." *CL* 26, no. 4 (August 1914): 46–47.

W. M. "Practical Details of Bird Gardens." *CL* 26, no. 4 (August 1914): 74.

Practical Help on Landscape Gardening. University of Illinois Agricultural Experiment Station Circular no. 176 (Urbana, October 1914).

"Shrubs for a Small Lot." *Country Gentleman* 79, no. 41 (10 October 1914): 32.

"'Landscape Extension' in the Middle West." *GM* 21, no. 1 (February 1915): 42–44.

"A Message to Old Friends." *GM* 21, no. 1 (February 1915): 11.

"Landscape Forestry and Wild Gardening Increase the Beauty and Value of the Farm." *Craftsman* 27, no. 6 (March 1915): 650–59, 694.

"Views Are Worth More Than Trees." *CL* 27, no. 5 (March 1915): 56–58.

Wilhelm Miller, L. E. Foglesong, and Franz A. Aust. "Western Perennials for Western Gardens." In *The Standard Cyclopedia of Horticulture*, edited by L. H. Bailey. Vol. 3, 1469–71. New York: Macmillan, 1915.

Wilhelm Miller and Franz A. Aust. "Planting a Corner Lot." *Country Gentleman* 80, no. 18 (1 May 1915): 18–20.

"Some Inspiring Examples of Roadside Planting." *Billerica: North Shore Illinois Edition* 6, no. 2, pt. 2 (July 1915): 4–7.

The Prairie Spirit in Landscape Gardening. University of Illinois Agricultural Experiment Station Circular no. 184 (Urbana, November 1915).

"Landscape Extension." In *The Standard Cyclopedia of Horticulture*, edited by L. H. Bailey. Vol. 4, 1813–16. New York: Macmillan, 1916.

"The Minnesota Spirit in Landscape Gardening." *Minnesotan* 1, no. 7 (February 1916): 7–13.

"The Prairie Spirit in Landscape Gardening." *American City* 14, no. 2 (February 1916): 135–38.

"The First Roadside Planting along the Lincoln Highway." *American City* 14, no. 4 (April 1916): 325–29.

"Belt Planting." *CL* 30, no. 4 (August 1916): 28–29.

"The Prairie Spirit in Landscape Gardening." *American Magazine of Art* 7, no. 11 (September 1916): 448–50.

"Foundation Planting." *GM* 24, no. 3 (October 1916): 86–88.

"The Prairie Style of Landscape Architecture." *Architectural Record* 40, no. 6 (December 1916): 590–92.

"The Use of Roses in the Landscape." In *The American Rose Annual: The 1917 Yearbook of Rose Progress*, edited by J. Horace McFarland. Vol. 2, 12–15. Harrisburg, Pa.: American Rose Society, 1917.

"'Ragtime' Gardening—and Something Better." *Minnesotan* 2, no. 9 (March 1917): 28–29.

"Planting for Privacy of the Home." *GM* 25, no. 3 (April 1917): 169–70.

William Tyler Miller. "Shrubs and Vines for California Gardens." *GM* 32, no. 4 (December 1920): 191–93.

Circular 184   ILLINOIS AGRICULTURAL EXPERIMENT STATION   November, 1915

The Prairie Spirit in Landscape Gardening

WHAT THE PEOPLE OF ILLINOIS HAVE DONE AND CAN DO TOWARD DESIGNING AND PLANTING PUBLIC AND PRIVATE GROUNDS FOR EFFICIENCY AND BEAUTY

By WILHELM MILLER

Department of Horticulture, Division of Landscape Extension

A forerunner of a prairie type of permanent farm home surrounded by permanent vegetation native to Illinois

UNIVERSITY OF ILLINOIS
COLLEGE OF AGRICULTURE
URBANA

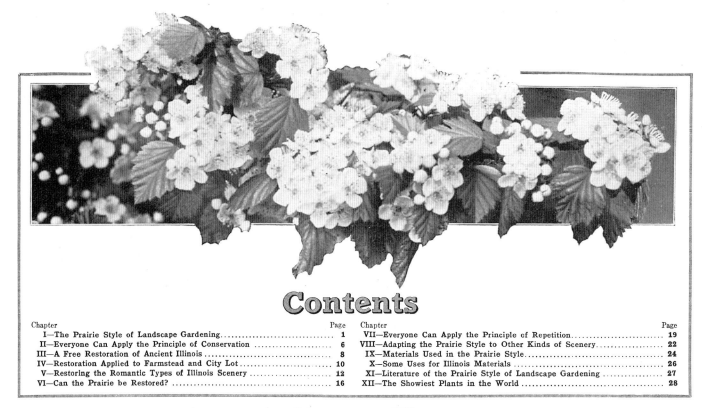

Contents

"DONE IN ILLINOIS"

The above words, accompanied by a bur-oak leaf, have been inserted inconspicuously in the lower corners of many photographs as a guarantee that the pictures were really taken in Illinois and not in other states and represent cultivation rather than wild nature. All such pictures are examples of the "Illinois way of planting," since they contain a high percentage of trees and shrubs native to Illinois. Many of these landscape effects have been consciously designed in the prairie style of landscape gardening. Collectively these pictures offer convincing evidence that Illinois is creating a new and appropriate type of beauty.

"Conservation" is the First Principle of the Prairie Style of Landscape Gardening

Has your community destroyed its oldest trees or has it saved its scenery, like Riverside? These trees line a river bank, which is not treated as a dump-heap, while the elders and sumacs show that the lot owners save and encourage in their back yards the luxuriant, native vegetation.

Chicago Public Library
Rogers Park Branch

Customer ID: ********2450

Items that you checked out

Title:
 The prairie spirit of landscape gardening
ID: R0303059970
Due: Monday, June 12, 2023

Total items: 1
Account balance: $0.00
5/22/2023 1:05 PM

Items that you already have on loan

Title:
 Your Biblical garden : plants of the Bible
 and how to grow them
ID: R0008273217
Due: Wednesday, June 14, 2023

Thank you for using the Chicago Public
Library.

I---The Prairie Style of Landscape Gardening

A New Mode of Designing and Planting, Which Aims to Fit the Peculiar Scenery, Climate, Soil, Labor, and Other Conditions of the Prairies, Instead of Copying Literally the Manners and Materials of Other Regions

THE Middle West is just beginning to evolve a new style of architecture, interior decoration, and landscape gardening, in an effort to create the perfect home amid the prairie states. This movement is founded on the fact that one of the greatest assets which any country or natural part of it can have, is a strong national or regional character, especially in the homes of the common people. Its westernism grows out of the most striking peculiarity of middle-western scenery, which is the prairie, i. e., flat or gently rolling land that was treeless when the white man came to Illinois. Some of the progress that has been made toward a prairie style of architecture is incidentally illustrated in these pages. (See front cover, and Figs. 1, 5, 17, and 76.)

The progress in landscape gardening is typified by the following statement from one member of the new "middle-western school of artists: "When I was landscape gardener for the West Side parks in Chicago I directed the expenditure of nearly $4,000,000 on projects inspired by the prairie. Some of the money went for salaries and maintenance, but there was a bond issue of $3,000,000 for new construction. This was chiefly spent on such designs as the Prairie River in Humboldt Park (Fig. 2), the Prairie Rose-garden (Fig. 8), and the Conservatories in Garfield Park (Figs. 25-34). Of course, the primary motive was to give recreation and pleasure to the people, but the secondary motive was to inspire them with the vanishing beauty of the prairie. Therefore, I used many symbols of the prairie, i. e., plants with strongly horizontal branches or flower clusters that repeat in obvious or subtle ways the horizontal line of land and sky which is the most impressive phenomenon on the boundless plains. Also, I aimed to re-create the atmosphere of the prairie by restoring as high a proportion as possible of the trees, shrubs, and flowers native to Illinois."

The principles of design on which the "prairie men" lay most stress are conservation, restoration, and repetition, as illustrated on the contents page and by Figs. 2 and 3.

A great field for applying these principles is offered by our parks. Of course, literal restoration of prairie scenery is impractical in places that are visited by thousands of people daily. But the spirit of truth can be restored to every large city park in the Middle West, witness the Prairie River and its adjacent meadow (Fig. 2). Each city can produce a different picture by restoring its local color, or characteristic vegetation. There are three ways of doing this, for the prairie spirit can be idealized, conventionalized, or symbolized. For example, it is idealized in the Conservatories (Figs. 25-34) by suggesting the appearance of Illinois in geological periods before the coming of man. It is conventionalized in the Rose-garden (Fig. 8) so much so that there are no prairie flowers in it, and in Humboldt boulevard (Fig. 59). It is symbolized in the playground at Douglas Park (Figs. 55-56) by means of plants with horizontal branches and flower clusters.

The same principles and methods have been used on many private estates, which offer a larger canvas for pure restorations than the average farmstead or city lot. However, every home can express the new idea in proportion to its means. The farmer may idealize his farm view by fram-

1. The Prairie Style of Landscape Gardening Married to the Prairie Style of Architecture

"The environment is woodland," says the landscape architect, "but the newly planted crab apples are designed to frame the view of the house and give an invitation to the prairie which is not far away." (Home of Henry Babson, River Forest; Louis H. Sullivan, architect.)

2. "Restoration" Is the Second Principle in the Prairie Style

The aim is to re-create the spirit of disappearing types of American scenery by restoring as much as possible of the "local color" or peculiar character impressed upon each scenic unit by nature thru ages of experiment. The famous "Prairie River" in Humboldt Park, Chicago. (Jens Jensen, landscape architect.)

ing it with haws as in Fig. 12. The city dweller may conventionalize the prairie in his garden, as in Fig. 13. The humblest renter may symbolize the prairie by putting a prairie rose beside the door, as in Fig. 14. Amid the most artificial surroundings it is possible to hint at the bountiful prairie which surrounds every city and is the source of its prosperity. Even among the tenements, a single brown-eyed daisy in a window box may keep alive the hope of freedom, prosperity, and a life amid more beautiful surroundings. Thus every home in Illinois can connect itself with the greatest source of inspiration in middle-western scenery, by preserving, restoring, or repeating some phase of the prairie.

The origin of the "middle-western movement" in landscape gardening, if it may be so called, can be traced back to 1878 when Mr. Bryan Lathrop "discovered" Mr. O. C. Simonds and persuaded him to become a landscape gardener. The latter then began to lay out the new part of Graceland Cemetery, which, during the next quarter of a century, was perhaps the most famous example of landscape gardening designed by a western man. It is more than a mere cemetery, for it is full of spiritual suggestion, and its wonderful effects produced by trees and shrubs native to Illinois have profoundly influenced the planting of home grounds. In 1880 Mr. Simonds began to transplant from the wilds the common Illinois species of oak, maple, ash, hornbeam, pepperidge, thorn apple, witch hazel, panicled dogwood, sheepberry, elder, and the like. Many of these plants have achieved great size and beauty. All the species named are nowadays called "stratified plants," but there was no talk then of "repetition," or even of "restoration." The guiding spirit was that respect for the quieter beauties of native vegetation which comes to every cultured person after he has lived a few years among the showiest plants from all foreign lands as assembled in ordinary nurseries and in the front yards of beginners. Graceland was to be a place of rest and peace, not a museum or a gaudy show. Should not the same ideal prevail in our home grounds?

The first piece of work done by Mr. Simonds that suggests what is now called "restoration," was begun in 1895 at Quincy, Illinois, when its famous park system overlooking the Mississippi was projected under the leadership of the late Edward J. Parker. One glance at the plans shows that Mr. Simonds had drunk deep of the spirit of Downing and the elder Olmsted, who taught that preservation of the natural landscape is usually more beautiful and less costly than leveling every hill and filling every ravine. Some of the best-known work of Mr. Simonds is in Lincoln Park, Chicago, but the whole "North Shore" shows his influence in home grounds.

Probably the first designer who consciously took the prairie as a leading motive is Mr. Jens Jensen, who was trained in Denmark and came to America in 1883. In 1885 he settled in Chicago and was at once impressed by the surrounding prairie, which was then a sea of grasses and flowers. Acres of phlox and

3. "Repetition" is the Third Principle in the Prairie Style of Landscape Gardening.

The branches or flowers of hawthorns repeat many times on a small scale the horizontal line of land or sky, which is often the strongest feature of middle-western scenery. Every flat flower cluster is a symbol of the prairie. Graceland Cemetery, Chicago, has greatly influenced home planting in Illinois. (O. C. Simonds, landscape gardener.)

4-5. Can We Make out of Simple Scenery and Common Plants a Prairie Style of Architecture and Landscape Gardening?

Beside the barbed-wire or occasional rail fences of Illinois, the farmer sometimes leaves a relic of "the glory that was," some "repeater of the prairie," i. e., a harmless shrub with flat flower clusters, like elder, dogwood, or viburnum.

"I purposely repeated the prairie line in the roofs," says the architect, William Drummond. "The elder in the back yard echoes the same note. It suggests that this house would look more homelike with foundation planting."

blazing star and thousands of compass plants were a familiar sight. The first design in which prairie flowers were used in a large, impressive way, was made in 1901 for Mr. Chalmers at Lake Geneva. Here were planted hundreds of the wild Phlox paniculata, parent of more than 400 garden varieties; hundreds of purple flags (Iris versicolor) collected from the banks of the Desplaines river, and hundreds of swamp rose mallows which glorify the rivers of Illinois in August with their pink flowers five inches in diameter. The first attempt to epitomize the beauty of Illinois rivers was made in 1901 for Mr. Harry Rubens at Glencoe, where there are a miniature spring, brook, waterfall, and lake (Figs. 47-48). Practically all the surrounding trees, shrubs, and flowers were planted, and more than ninety-five percent of the species grow wild within a mile of the spot. From 1905 to 1907 he designed and planted the Prairie River and Prairie Rose-garden in Humboldt Park, and the Conservatories in Garfield Park.

A third landscape architect who has been greatly influenced by the prairie is Walter Burley Griffin. He received his training in landscape gardening at the University of Illinois, and supplemented it by work in the offices of several

architects of the western school. He planned many houses in the prairie style. His chief American work in landscape architecture has been done at DeKalb, Decatur, Oak Park, Hubbard's Woods, Edwardsville, and Veedersburg, Indiana. The planting list for DeKalb shows that as early as 1906 he was using a high percentage of plants native to Illinois—especially the stratified materials. In 1912 he won a world-competition for a city plan for Canberra, the new capital of Australia. Mr. Griffin must be regarded as a middle-western landscape architect, since he maintains an office in Illinois and undertakes new work in the Middle West.

There are many other good landscape gardeners now practicing in the Middle West. Those who acknowledge the prairie as a leading motive in their work, are, however, not numerous at the time this paper is prepared. There are several young men whose work is promising, but not mature or extensive enough to show their feeling for the prairie style. One of the older men has submitted an itemized list of his work in the prairie style done in Illinois and nearby states since 1901 which makes the respectable total of $6,000,000.

Whether the work here described and illustrated consti-

6. A Farm View without a Frame of Trees

Altho corn is considered one of the most beautiful crops, people often complain that Illinois scenery is tame and monotonous. The wild prairie, with its varied flowers, has gone forever. How can men restore flowers and poetic suggestion to a land nearly ninety percent of which is tilled?

7. A Farm View Framed by Hawthorns in Bloom

The farmer can increase the natural beauty of his pasture or cornfields by planting trees near his front door, beside the dining-room window, along the road, or wherever he can frame a good view. Especially suitable are stratified trees, like haws, crabs, honey locust, and flowering dogwood.

8. The Prairie Style can be Executed in the Formal Manner

This rose garden in Humboldt Park is so conventionalized that it contains no prairie flowers. "But," says the designer, "I put hawthorns at the entrance to suggest the meeting of woods and prairie. Also I lowered the garden two feet in order to get the flowers well below the level of the eye as they are on the prairie in the spring. I gave the people the obvious beauty of roses and I hope a subtle charm also."

them as the formal and informal manners. For example, the prairie style has been executed in the formal manner, as in the Rose-garden (Fig. 8), tho it is generally executed in the informal manner. Authoritative books commonly speak of the 'garden-esque style,' which is typified by canna beds in the middle of the lawn. Surely all the middle-western work is better than that, and even the most conservative examples are colored more or less by middle-western materials. For these reasons I am willing to accept 'the prairie style of landscape gardening' (a phrase which I did not propose) until a better name for this new thing is discovered and agreed upon."

The settlement of this amicable difference of opinion we leave to our readers. Whether the new work is good or bad, time alone can tell. Perhaps the publication of this circular should have been postponed a century

tutes a new style or not is an interesting and important question. One of the conservative group among the middle-western landscape gardeners says, "I doubt if there is any western style of art. Good design must always grow out of the necessities peculiar to each case—not out of pet theories. I am not conscious of any new principles of design." As to motives, of course, the creator of an artwork is the final authority, but as to results the general public is entitled to an opinion. The popular belief is that the man just quoted has a style of his own, and that his work also possesses an indefinable quality that may be called middle-western. He generally uses a rather large proportion of western plants—more than most eastern landscape gardeners who have done important work in Illinois.

When the same question was put to one of the progressive or prairie group he replied: "Undoubtedly there is a middle-western style of landscape gardening. All good design that meets western conditions counts toward a western style. Style, according to Webster, is a characteristic or peculiar mode of developing an idea or accomplishing a result. The conservatives unconsciously use, to some extent, conservation, restoration, and repetition. The middle-western work is not a 'style' in the same sense that people speak of the 'formal and informal styles.' It would be more accurate to speak of

or two. On the other hand, the average person has a strange disinclination to wait a hundred years for the news. The people of Illinois actually seem glad to know about a new thing before it is too late for them to benefit by it. And they are generally willing to assume full responsibility for their own opinions. We do not advise any one style of architecture or landscape gardening for all conditions, nor have we any quarrel with those who prefer older styles of architecture and gardening. All we ask is that every reader see some of the new work for himself, with a mind free from prejudice.

Symbol of the Illinois Way—Illinois or Prairie Rose.

Definition of the "Illinois Way"

The Illinois way of planting is not a new system of design. The original definition says, "The Illinois way is to meet all the outdoor needs of the family by having ninety percent of the planting composed of trees and shrubs that grow wild in Illinois." However, in the most exacting and artificial conditions, like downtown parks, formal gardens, and the smallest city yard, only ten to twenty percent of Illinois plants may be consistent with good design.

9-10. Before and After Restoring the Native Flora to a Man-Made Watercourse in Humboldt Park

"This bank had been denuded of its original vegetation," says the designer. "The margin did not look as bad as this, because it was grassed, but it was not redeemed by a single tree, shrub, or flower. The location is identified by a good old cottonwood in the park and an exclamatory Lombardy poplar, which I spared in a moment of weakness. I shall be glad when the poplar dies, for it cuts like a knife thru the billowy masses of western woodland."

Around the foundations of the ordinary house, forty to fifty percent may be suitable, while the borders may contain sixty to ninety percent of Illinois species with general satisfaction. Therefore, the following revised definition is proposed: "The Illinois way of planting is to use as high a proportion of plants native to Illinois as is consistent with practical requirements and the principles of design." In this sense, our neighboring states may have an Iowa or Indiana way, using the same plants that we do, for there is no plant of importance native to Illinois that is not also native to other prairie states. And, by the same method, every state in the Union can develop a beauty of its own, even if no state is a scenic unit.

Definition of the "Prairie Style"

The prairie style of landscape gardening, however, is a genuine style in the opinion of several critics, for it is based on a geographic, climatic, and scenic unit, and it employs three accepted principles of design—conservation of native scenery, restoration of local vegetation, and repetition of a dominant line. However, it is not a system of rules and there never can be anything of the sort in any fine art, tho people crave it forever. In good design there are only principles. Nor is the prairie style a mere collection of novel features, such as campfires, players' greens, council hills, prairie gardens, and Illinois borders. Features never make a style. Sundials, pergolas, and blue spruces may fit certain conditions to perfection, but a man who uses them in every plan is open to the suspicion of being an inferior designer. Therefore, until something better can be had, the following definition is proposed: The prairie style of landscape gardening is an American mode of design based upon the practical needs of the middle-western people and characterized by preservation of typical western scenery, by restoration of local color, and by repetition of the horizontal line of land or sky which is the strongest feature of prairie scenery.

To those who are in danger of being carried away by new fashions, may we give a word of caution? The best gardens cannot be had simply for paying money and copying or imitating. One must patiently study fundamental principles. There is nothing new about the principles used in the prairie style; only their applications are new. Some even declare that the only new thing in the world is undying zeal for hard, persistent work in adapting old principles to new conditions. Surely there is no other way to produce that thing which is infinitely more precious than the universal, endless imitation of the past— a living national art which grows out of the heart of the people and which the humblest mortal can understand and enjoy, as every Greek did in the thrilling new days when temples and statues were growing out of the rock at Athens!

In the great work of fitting homes to the prairie country every one of us may have a part, for everyone may strive towards a permanent home surrounded by permanent native plants. Let us do all we can to help realize an Illinois type of farmhouse married to an Illinois type of interior decoration and landscape gardening.

11. The Minnesota Model Farmhouse

Plans secured (1913) by Minnesota State Art Society, published by University of Minnesota, St. Paul, in Extension Bulletin 52. Who will help Illinois develop an Illinois type of farmhouse set in a farmstead designed for efficiency and beauty?

Note on Chapter Endings

To meet the ever-recurring question, "What shall we do?" we have put, at the ends of certain chapters, summaries in the form of practical suggestions headed by the phrase "I will" or "We will." The former is a motto of Chicago; the latter has been suggested as a new, informal motto for Illinois. Is your family united on any of the projects named below? If not, the "We will" suggestions may help you agree on what you wish to do. Again, to realize one's ideal it is often helpful to record one's aim. If you wish to record an individual determination or family agreement you may make a cross in the appropriate square. Such action commits nobody to any expense or publicity. It is merely a private memorandum.

WE WILL

☐ See some of the chief works of the western landscape gardeners.
☐ Have a landscape gardener make a comprehensive design for our home grounds.
☐ Draw to scale a plan for our farmstead or city lot and get the best advice we can.
☐ Connect with the "Illinois way" by putting in our front yard at least one mass of shrubs native to Illinois.
☐ Study some of the best "prairie houses," indoors and out, with a mind free from prejudice.
☐ Build a farmhouse or country home in prairie style.

Symbol of the Prairie Style —A Stratified Hawthorn.

12-14. Three Ways by which Every Illinoisan can Bring the Prairie Spirit into his Home Grounds in Country or City

12. Idealize the farm view, e. g., frame it with haws, crabs, or honey locust.
13. Conventionalize the prairie, e. g., put into the formal garden some flat-topped flowers.
14. Symbolize the prairie, e. g., plant Illinois or prairie roses beside the front door.

15-16. Is your Community Butchering its Trees, or is it Saving them as Urbana Does?

The elms at the right and all other street trees in Urbana are being saved by a public-spirited citizen, who serves as "tree warden" without pay. No one can cut down, prune, or plant a tree without his permission. Cannot your community have a city forester or shade-tree commission?

II—Everyone Can Apply the Principle of Conservation

IT WILL do little good to bewail the beauty that has been destroyed in Illinois. Let us save the beauty that is left. Here is a simple program that may help every reader decide what he can do for this great cause.

1. Save the trees on your home grounds. Have a tree surgeon examine them and estimate the cost of putting them in perfect condition. Locate the new house so as to save trees (see Figs. 17 and 76). Let every farmer save a few trees for shade and beauty, even if they do harm crops a little. For example, save some trees along the roadside, around the farmstead, near the barns, and at least one tree in the permanent pasture. See Figs. 19-20.

2. Help save the street trees. Take the trees out of politics and put them in charge of a public-spirited citizen serving without pay —a city forester, or tree warden (see Figs. 15-16). He can stop tree butchery caused by telegraph and telephone companies.

3. Help save roadside trees and shrubs. See your township supervisor or county superintendent of highways. Show him Figs. 21 to 24 and 51 to 54.

4. Help save the watercourses. Get the authorities to forbid their use as dumping grounds (see contents page).

5. Help save the historic features of your community and give them a proper setting. See Fig. 18.

6. Help save the state's scenery. Join an organization that works for state reservations, like White Pine Grove, Cahokia Mounds, and the proposed addition to Starved Rock.

Organizations Devoted to Conservation

ON LOCAL propositions it is generally best to work thru the Chamber of Commerce or the Woman's Club.

The National Conservation Association, of which Gifford Pinchot is president, is devoted to saving our natural resources, especially the forests, waterways, and minerals. The secretary is Harry A. Slattery, Colorado building, Washington, D. C.

The American Civic Association, of which J. Horace McFarland is president, is devoted largely to city planning, including housing. It has issued important publications on smoke, billboards, saving Niagara, and other subjects. The secretary is Richard Watrous, 913 Union Trust building, Washington, D. C.

The Friends of Our Native Landscape, of which Jens Jensen is president, aim to save all types of native scenery by means of national, state, and local reservations. The secretary is Sherman M. Booth, Borland building, Chicago.

The General Federation of Woman's Clubs has a Conservation Department with committees on forestry (including street trees, waterways, birds, and Lincoln Highway). The chairman of the Conservation Department is Mrs. John Dickinson Sherman, Hyde Park Hotel, Chicago.

The Illinois Federation of Woman's Clubs has a Conservation Department, the chairman of which is Mrs. Charles W. Irion, Ottawa, Illinois.

I WILL

☐ Write to national, state, and local organizations interested in conservation, study their literature, and help them all I can.

☐ Work and vote for the extension of the state park system to include all types of Illinois scenery.

☐ Ask the county highway superintendent to save trees, shrubs, and flowers on state and country roadsides.

☐ Work and vote to help our community extend its system of local parks and reservations, and to save the street trees.

☐ Give the people some piece of scenery to enjoy forever.

☐ Save the permanent native vegetation on my farm or home grounds, as far as possible.

17. Let us Save the Trees on our Home Grounds

"Because I love trees I bought this lot and snuggled my house among them, so that three big trees are growing thru the front porch. I cut a hole in the eaves to make room for one."—William Drummond, River Forest.

18. Save Every Historic Feature and Give It a Proper Setting!

"Lincoln often slept in this century-old cabin—the first built in Piatt county. We moved it to an environment like the original. Many old settlers' cabins are now preserved in parks and more should be."—William F. Lodge, Monticello.

19-20. Have you sent your Woodlot to the Sawmill, or have you Saved it?

"Here is the sawmill with which I cut up my neighbors' trees, but not my own. If they insist on selling their birthright, I might as well have some of the pottage. But before I accept a job I remind my neighbor that for three generations my family has never cut a tree on our farm, just because they are beautiful. And the fourth generation promises to do the same. At the right are some of our trees."—L. D. Seass, Arthur, Illinois.

21-22. Have you Saved the "Brush" along the Roadside?

Farmers, will you reduce your daily drive to this condition or do you want something in your life besides dollars? You can save beauty that would cost you $500 to $1,500 a mile to replace by conference with your highway superintendent or county supervisor. The Illinois law does not compel the cutting of brush, only of *noxious weeds*. These sumacs have been saved by Wisconsin people along a famous drive into Madison.

23-24. Have you Saved the Trees along the Roadside for Shade and Beauty?

These ash trees at the left were cut down for the usual reason, "they harmed ten rows of corn." The trees at the right have been preserved near Sidell by getting every supervisor to agree not to cut them down. Trees in the middle of a road have great educational value because they compel attention.

III—A Free Restoration of Ancient Illinois

A SERIES OF LANDSCAPES UNDER GLASS, SUGGESTING THE BEAUTY OF VANISHED AND DISAPPEARING TYPES OF SCENERY

PARK design is an important part of landscape gardening, and a popular feature in every large park system is a range of greenhouses. The famous Conservatories in Garfield Park, Chicago, have attracted hundreds of thousands of visitors and have been pronounced the "best of the kind in the world." Prior to 1906 the West Side had three small, old-fashioned greenhouses in separate parks. These buildings were visited by few persons and could hardly be said to adorn the scenery. The new landscape gardener proposed to destroy them in favor of one great new structure in which Chicagoans could take real pride. At first the project was resisted, for no locality likes to lose any permanent improvement, but when the plans were explained, the people became enthusiastic.

Instead of the customary potted plants on high benches we are surprised to find these nature-like gardens. The most intelligent visitors are deeply moved by these exquisite scenes and feel that they convey an idea too deep for words. This intuition is correct, for the designer's motive is restoration. His pictures do not pretend to furnish a literal, scientific restoration of any particular geological epoch, such as a museum might have. The idea is poetical—to suggest the tropical beauty of prairie-land before the coming of man. And the reason for this is that we need to see our surroundings from a fresh point of view. We need to realize that modern Illinois contains equally beautiful scenery that we thoughtlessly destroy, but ought to save or restore.

Few communities in Illinois can afford greenhouses large enough for such landscapes under glass, but they all have a great opportunity out-of-doors. Every large park can preserve or re-create one epitome of the scenery and vegetation of Illinois.

Can you not apply the principle of restoration to your own home grounds? These pictures should stimulate your imagination. If you have room for only one bush to symbolize the vanished scenery, may we suggest the prairie rose? See also pages 24, 25.

25. The First Spring in Prairie-Land

This man-made rockwork is so successful that visitors commonly believe that it is a natural spring, around which the greenhouse was built.

26. First Cascade in First Prairie River

Perhaps it stepped down then as now, with giant ferns, like the golden polypody arching over the cliffs like falling water.

26a. A Man-Made Cascade in Kentucky

One of the many ways in which the restoration spirit expresses itself out-of-doors. This is forty-two inches high and cost about $40.

27. When Chicago was a Jungle

The first greenhouse contains a long vista like a tunnel lined with palms and ferns. At the end is this fountain, which alternately leaps and disappears.

28. The First Hint of Stratification, or Repetition of the Prairie Line

Tropical evergreens, like Norfolk Island pines or araucarias, may have sounded the note now echoed by white pines beside Lake Michigan and hawthorns on the prairie. The rocks of this primitive watercourse are horizontally stratified like the St. Peter sandstone of some prairie rivers of today.

29. Some Ancient River Bluff or Rolling Prairie

When the forest may have been composed of tree ferns and fringed with Venus' hair, forerunner of our matchless hardy maidenhair. Let us restore to woodlots and river banks the overhanging bushes and ferns that form the most picturesque and romantic element in middle-western scenery!

30. Nature's First Dream of Prairie-Land

This open, central lawn (one of the fundamental conceptions of landscape gardening out-of-doors) is not composed of vertical grass blades. To give the prairie feeling the designer used a moss-like plant with stratified foliage—Selaginella denticulata. In Fig. 25 he used the moisture-loving S. Martensii.

31. The Original Woodland Border

Not like the stark southern pine forests where there is no undergrowth to soften the abrupt descent from tall trees to flat meadow. The transition from forest to prairie made by haws and crabs should be the motive of our hardy borders.

32. The Primitive Glade in a Middle-Western Forest

Half-close the eyes, and the hard brick walk becomes the winding trail that leads to woodland mysteries, hinting of primeval campfires, council rocks, and players' greens. Forest and prairie subtly connected by stratified maidenhair.

33. The Beginning of a Prairie Bog

Here are water hyacinth, cardamon, umbrella plant, and the palm-like curculigo. In modern bogs grow orchids, pitcher plants, and fringed gentian. Shall we save no moist spot near each community where future generations may enjoy the unique flowers of bog gardens?

34. The Margin of some Ancient "Lake Illinois"

When tropical plants arched over the bank, as do these tree ferns, cardamon, and Nephrolepis. Let us put this grace into hardy water gardens by planting the Cornus stolonifera, Typha angustifolia, and Calamagrostis of the prairie rivers.

35-36. The Kind of Restoration that costs the Farmer not one Cent—only the Labor of Collecting and Planting Waterside Flowers

The cattle must have a place to drink, but why not restore to some creeks the original margin of shrubs and perennials? The first picture typifies the "early goose pond" style of treating water in city parks. The second shows a restoration in an Illinois city park. (Pickerel weed and calamus.)

IV—Restoration Applied to Farmstead and City Lot

EVEN WHEN LITTLE MONEY AND SPACE ARE AVAILABLE, EVERYONE CAN APPLY THE PRINCIPLE OF RESTORATION

THE aim of restoration is to re-create as much of the local scenery or vegetation as is practical. Like every other great idea, restoration can be expressed in some way by everyone. No matter how humble the individual or how crude the expression, the effort is worth while because it is one's own experience and not another's. On one square foot of ground a child expresses his love of country in a map of sand, epitomizing the whole United States by using pebbles for mountains, maple seedlings for forests, and a little real water for the Great Lakes and the Mississippi. This effort means more to the child than a better map made or bought for him by others. So, too, every "grown-up" in Illinois can apply the principles of landscape gardening. The popular notion that landscape gardening is only for city parks and the wealthy few is a great mistake. Of course, the grandest public examples involve much space and cost, but so far as self-expression goes, landscape gardening offers as great an opportunity to every living soul as music does, or any other fine art. The one principle that everyone can apply is restoration.

For example, take the two extreme cases of the people who have no money and those who have no land. The farm laborer goes to the woods, digs up an unknown bush or vine and plants it beside his tenant cottage. To him it may suggest the fatherland from which he has just come, or the child on whose birthday it was planted, or the place he likes to go on Sunday afternoons. It is a crude expression of the manifold charms of Illinois woodland, but to this immigrant it is a step toward naturalization, perhaps even the beginning of wisdom. Moreover, real beauty is there for everyone to see and enjoy. The country folk pause and think: "Life is not all corn and hogs—to him."

On the other hand, the city merchant may have plenty of money, but not one foot of earth in front of his store. Let us assume that he is tired of the artificial surroundings and goes to the country for a day's rest and change. And, while there, an idea comes to him—he will have something more permanent and natural than window boxes. He will have vines—the kind he used to like as a boy on the farm, the narrow-leaved "woodbine," a

variety of Virginia creeper so common in Illinois that, for purposes of sentiment, we may call it the "Illinois creeper." He has two holes cut in the concrete sidewalk, and plants his souvenirs of Illinois. To him they may recall the parents that are gone, or they may remind him of "the day" when he is to shut up shop for good and retire to a country home. The passers-by know nothing of all this, but they are glad to see some sign of country beauty in the city. They say, "Life is not all dollars to that man."

Can such simple plantings be called "restorations" in any important sense? Certainly, if they honestly express the individual's love of the local scenery, combined with his love of home, and town, and state. Restoration is fundamentally an act of the spirit; the scale of operations is incidental. If there is space or money available only for a pair of Illinois roses beside the front door, anything more is pretense. The essential thing is to plant some permanent reminder of the native beauty, and the cost should always be well within one's means. A person may

37-38. Scene of a Woodlot Restoration in Vermilion County, where the Aim is Typified by these Illinois Bluebells

"Like many other farmers, I must plead guilty to harming the beauty of woodlots by cutting out shrubs and letting animals destroy the flowers. But I am now restocking this grove. This process costs a good deal more than saving the original ground-cover. Since I have no business but farming and live on the farm the year round, I feel that my family is entitled to some of the enjoyments that can be had only in the country."—Harvey J. Sconce, Sidell, Illinois.

prefer to have foreign plants in his garden but he must care enough about the native kinds to plant some of them in the public part of his property. For restoration means more than mere gardening—more than the planting of double roses and lilacs, the beauty of which everyone can see. The "restorer" must prove that he wants to be surrounded by common, native things, rather than by rare and costly foreigners.

Is such restoration of any value to the public? Undoubtedly. Even if the results were wholly subjective and individual they would be worth while because everyone is better for making some harmless expression of an unselfish ideal. But the results are evident to all! The Illinois rose beside the door is beautiful in itself and every year it will come to mean more to every passer-by because it will suggest pleasant thoughts of Illinois. Everyone will know that it is put there not to display wealth, but in the pure spirit of restoration. Everyone will know that it is not intended to deceive, for no bush can imitate the prairie, and no person can ever mistake a tree for a forest. But, every year, more people accept the stratified bush or flat-topped flower as a symbol of the prairie and therefore of peace, freedom, and plenty. Every year more people accept the prairie rose as a symbol of the "Prairie State" of Illinois. When people see that rose in your yard, their eyes brighten and their manner says, "It is for Illinois. You have restored something of her native beauty."

What the Average Farmer Can Restore

THE ordinary farmer has little time, labor, or knowledge of design and ornamental plants, but he has two immense advantages—plenty of room (often 160 acres), and a chance to collect wild shrubs and flowers. Starting with no cash outlay and a day's work in the fall, he can accomplish eventually ten things.

1. *Foundation planting.* He can make the house look like a home by moving some shrubs from the woods.
2. *Screens.* He can hide part of the barnyard and out-buildings, at least from his windows.
3. *Views.* He can frame the view of his house from the road and the best view of his farm from the house by transplanting a pair of red haws. See Fig. 7.
4. *The border.* He can enclose the farmstead with an irregular border of shrubbery that will give more year-round beauty than a hedge, trimmed or untrimmed.
5. *The farmstead.* He can plant the whole farmstead to meet the above-named needs of the family, as well as shade, playground, laundry yard, etc.

6. *The creek.* He can restore some of the marginal vegetation. See Figs. 35, 36.
7. *The woodlot.* He can restore many wild flowers simply by fencing a piece of woods. See Figs. 37, 38.
8. *Edges of fields.* He can attract the song birds that are friendly to his crops by planting at the edges or corners of one or more fields some native shrubs, especially the kinds that do not breed pests or rob the soil too much.
9. *Roadside.* He can plant beside the public road a few trees and some harmless shrubs and flowers, and he can often persuade the commissioner not to cut them down. See Figs. 51, 52.
10. *The whole farm.* By "planting the waste land to scenery" he can create a private park—not as showy as the millionaire's, but beautiful and appropriate.

Mr. Farmer, can you not take all or most of these steps in about five years? It may cost a good deal, but it will be worth while. You cannot transplant everything from the wild without expense. Surely you can see the wisdom of buying your Illinois species whenever nursery stock is better or cheaper than collected stock. You should also see the wisdom of getting the best advice and designs that you can afford—especially at the outset. All or most of these plantings may be acts of restoration, instead of copy work. If you use only foreign and artificial varieties your place will make a gaudy contrast with the country scenery. If you restore a high percentage of Illinois trees and shrubs your home will fit the landscape.

What the City Lot Owner Can Restore

THE renter in a city cannot afford to make costly permanent improvements, but the average owner of a city lot is justified in doing so. His great trouble is not about money (for we are assuming that everyone keeps within his means and takes his time to do these things), but he has less space than the farmer. On the other hand, he can give more time per year to ornamental gardening than the farmer, because he needs outdoor exercise after his day's work. Starting with no knowledge of horticulture, and with whatever leisure the gardening members of the family may have, the average lot owner can accomplish eventually about seven things.

1. *Foundation planting.* He can restore something of the Illinois vegetation, even in this exacting location, for example, by viburnum (Fig. 40), fragrant sumac, or prairie rose (Fig. 39).
2. *Screens.* He can hide some of the unsightly surroundings, such as high fence or

outhouse, by wild grape, trumpet creeper, common sumac, elder, and other Illinois plants that are sometimes considered rather coarse for the front of the house. See contents page and Figs. 4, 5.
3. *Views.* He can frame the view of his home, for example, by a pair of elms, haws, or prairie crab apples, or if he considers his house ugly, he can transform it by hiding much of it with vines.
4. *Boundaries.* He can enclose the back yard with an irregular border of native shrubs in variety, instead of with an artificial and monotonous privet hedge.
5. *Front yard.* He can help tie the whole street into a park by persuading the neighbors to plant "connecting shrubbery" from the front of one house to another.
6. *Parking.* He can restore old trees to good health thru tree surgeons; he can combine with his neighbors to get a uniform street tree at uniform distances, or plant low shrubbery. See back cover.
7. *Entire lot.* He can have a plan made for the whole property, arranging in good order all features. He can restore the birds, with the aid of shrubbery, especially the Illinois dogwoods and viburnums.

Every one of these acts can, and usually should be, an act of restoration in some degree. Every list of the most efficient plants may include some Illinois materials—a low percentage near the house, and a higher one at the boundaries.

There is little danger of carrying restoration too far in cities. The great danger is that all front yards will look too gaudy, because beginners tend to buy the showiest varieties, like blue Colorado spruce and golden elder. Consequently they often plant 90 to 100 percent of foreign varieties. The same percentage of native plants would be more restful. We do not ask anyone to deny himself any flower he likes—only to move to the back yard the things that rarely fit the front yard, for example, cut-leaved, weeping, variegated, and tropical plants. Everyone has a place of unquestioned privilege in the back yard, provided it is shut off from the public gaze, but the front yard is public. And the real question is, "Shall we have 90 to 100 percent foreigners, or shall we have a clear suggestion of Illinois such as a majority of native plants may give?"

WE WILL

☐ Restore native scenery or vegetation to our farm at some of the ten places mentioned above.

☐ Restore native vegetation to our city lot, at some of the seven places mentioned above.

39. Every Illinoisan can Restore some Prairie Roses
Literal restoration of scenery is, of course, impossible amid cramped and artificial surroundings, but each year more people accept the prairie rose as a symbol of the Prairie State.

40. Every Illinoisan can Restore some Illinois Viburnums
Each year more people accept the stratified bush or flat-topped flower as a symbol of the prairie. This is Viburnum pubescens. One of the best for foundation planting is Viburnum dentatum.

41-42. Before and after Restoring a Typical Creek and Ravine in Northeastern Illinois

This picture was taken only a few feet away from the next and shows that the ravine was nearly dry, as are most of the ravines along Lake Michigan, owing, as some assert, to drainage caused by dense population. Also the wild flowers had been destroyed by picnic parties.

The owners have restored canoeing for about 1,000 feet, using city water from three three-quarter-inch pipes. A dam retains the water, which does not evaporate rapidly, owing to the shade. They have planted many nursery-grown wild flowers. Home of Mr. and Mrs. Julius Rosenwald, Ravinia, Illinois.

V—Restoring the Romantic Types of Illinois Scenery

EIGHT TYPES OF PICTURESQUE SCENERY DIFFERENT FROM THE PRAIRIE, WITH EXAMPLES OF THEIR RESTORATION

ALL varieties of Illinois scenery can, for practical purposes, be resolved into nine types, of which the prairie is most important, since it probably affects the greatest number of homes. The eight other types may be regarded as foils to the prairie. They are the lake bluffs, ravines, river-banks, ponds, rocks, dunes, woods, and roadsides. The roadside, of course, is not a natural unit, but it is an asylum for the wild flowers, and it has immense possibilities for beauty thru planting. The beauty of the eight minor types is of the obvious and popular sort, because of their romantic or picturesque character. But the beauty of the prairie is harder to understand. It may be well for us to consider the eight minor types of scenery before we try to restore the prairie.

Restoration of the Lake Bluffs

OUTSIDE the great cities of Illinois the most valuable residential property, from the assessor's standpoint, is the shore of Lake Michigan—a great underlying cause of this value being scenery, especially the lake and the wooded ravines. The whole shore from Chicago to Wisconsin is,

broadly speaking, a steep, high, clay-bank that is continually being eaten away by the water. See Fig. 43. Fortunes have been spent to save these bluffs from further destruction, and tens of thousands of dollars have been spent on restoration schemes of every sort—the bluffs being generally thickly planted with trees and shrubs in great variety by dozens of private owners. "Unfortunately," writes E. L. Millard of Highland Park, "practically all places are still in the 'locust stage' of development, the locust being the best soil-binder at the start, but an unsightly tree owing to the attacks of borers. The highest type of beauty worked out by nature along this shore can be inferred from five priceless fragments at and near Lake Forest that should be preserved with reverential care forever. The supreme plants, in my opinion, are the white pine, red cedar, arborvitæ, and canoe birch. At my own place (see Fig. 65) I am beginning to destroy the locusts and all other plants foreign to the locality, as I believe the highest possible aim is to restore and intensify the peculiar beauty which nature adapted to the lake bluff by experiments on a scale so colossal that those which the ordinary multimillionaire

can encompass during a single lifetime sink into insignificance."

Restoration of the Ravines

THE immense popular appeal of the ravines has been fatal to their highest beauty. First, the ravines attracted many home-builders, who soon demanded storm sewers, and these, according to some authorities, carried away much of the water that formerly gave the effect of charming creeks. Second, the ravines attract great Sunday crowds from Chicago, and these have despoiled the ravines of wild flowers. Under such conditions, restoration may be impossible unless private places are closed to the public, except during certain hours when supervision can be provided. Perhaps the largest and most consistent restoration is that made by Mr. and Mrs. Julius Rosenwald of Ravinia. See Figs. 41, 42. Most of the communities between Evanston and Wisconsin aim to attract high-grade residents and to discourage factories. Obviously the ravines form one of the greatest natural assets, and the communities that formerly treated them as dumping grounds are gradually transforming them into public parks and reservations. Let the good work go on!

43-44. Many Restorations of the Lake Bluffs have been made North of Chicago

At the right is the Cyrus H. McCormick place, Lake Forest, where about 150 species, mostly natives, clothe the banks. This wide beach has been created by means of jetties and the willows in the foreground, which were originally planted at the limits of wave action. Warren H. Manning, landscape designer.

45. "Away with Gaudy Foreigners and Artificial Varieties!"

"This overgrown nursery in Humboldt Park," says the designer, "was full of brilliant 'best-sellers,' such as cut-leaved, weeping, and variegated shrubs. These may be jewels in themselves, but superb specimens of them can be seen everywhere and forever. Shall we turn the whole outdoor world into a museum?"

46. "Restore the Native Vegetation!"

"Mr. Corngrower, can you see beauty in your creek, even when there is not a single flower or striking form? If so, you understand why we swept away the showier vegetation of Fig. 45 and restored the simple beauty you often thoughtlessly destroy. If you destroy it, will your children stay on the farm?"

Restoration of the River Banks

EVERY Illinoisan knows about the three great rivers in which we have a share, the Mississippi, Wabash, and Illinois, but to realize the wonderful possibilities of our water system for use, recreation, and beauty one must see a map devoted entirely to our watercourses, showing how few and small are the areas which the people cannot reach by means of a ten-cent fare or an hour's ride in an automobile or a farm buggy. Many of these watercourses have been denuded or desecrated and all sorts of restorations have been made in various parts of the state. Perhaps the largest and most consistent restoration is the "Prairie River" in Humboldt Park, Chicago, which aims to epitomize or suggest the characteristic beauty of the Illinois rivers as a whole. See Fig. 2. The "river," which is man-made, is 1,650 feet long, and varies in width from 52 to 108 feet. It has several branches and some cascades, with rock-work modeled after that of the Rock river. See Circular 170, Fig. 105. The designer deliberately discarded all foreign materials (see Figs. 45, 46) because he was attempting to re-create a pure Illinois landscape. By so doing he denied himself many showy flowers which he believes are among the finest that can be used in ordinary landscape gardening. For example, he would not use pink or yellow water lilies in Fig. 2, because they would not be true to nature. Fortunately, we can see these beautiful foreign plants in every park, but faithful restorations of by-gone scenery are rare. Every property owner along a watercourse or drainage ditch may restore some trees, shrubs, or flowers. Every citizen has a chance to work and vote for restoration of watercourses in park and community plans.

Restoration of Ponds, Pools, and Lakes

WHILE Illinois is not as rich in small lakes as the states to her north, the total amount of still or slowly-moving waters is respectable. Moreover, many city

47-48. Restoration vs. Show, or Inspiration vs. Desecration

"I shall not allow any showy geraniums or other foreign flowers to spoil the composition made for the previous owner of my place—Mr. Harry Rubens. The aim was to re-create an Illinois water system in miniature—spring, brook, cascade, river, and lake. These pictures were taken before all the Illinois species were planted. The Japanese iris and geraniums were stop-gaps until wild iris and prairie phlox could be established."—James Simpson, Glencoe.

49-50.   This Formal Garden was Destroyed by the Owner in favor of a Restoration of the Rocks

W. A. Simms of Spring Station, Kentucky, has taken the rocks beneath his lawn and, with the aid of an Illinois designer, built a miniature water system to epitomize the beauty of the ravines. K. D. Alexander has restored to a natural ravine the rock-loving flowers of his own county. No foreign flowers are tolerated. The same stratified rocks are found in Illinois and the same methods are practical where rocks and ravines occur.

residents are glad to consider a small water garden, provided the expense for water can be kept well within their means. Perhaps the most consistent restoration of the Illinois water scenery on any private place is the one at Glencoe, at the home of Mr. James Simpson. See Fig. 48. The designer of this garden says, "I aimed to reproduce in miniature the atmosphere and characteristic vegetation of Illinois rivers as a whole, especially the watercourses of the ravine country, when the ravines were young." This has been done on a piece of land 240 feet long, and from 30 to 60 feet wide, or about one-fourth of an acre. Most of the large trees in Figs. 47 and 48 were there, but everything else has been planted, including the red cedars. Numerous restored ponds of the type shown in Fig. 48 have been made, for example, such as at River Forest by Henry Babson, and at Bloomington by Spencer Ewing.

Restoration of Rocks

ROCKS are so rare in Illinois that every visible ledge is likely to have decided value. F. O. Lowden, on his place near Oregon, Illinois, has some land bordering Rock river which makes rather tame scenery, in spite of noble woods, until you come to a bold headland about thirty feet high, the beauty of which is doubled by reflection in the water. A good landscape gardener will sacrifice a good many bushes or trees to expose a

rugged and picturesque ledge. Such an act may be called restoration, even if the vegetation be destroyed, because it restores to the scenery a dramatic element that has been hidden. Many property owners along the Rock and Illinois rivers can apply this principle, especially at river bends.

Most Illinoisans have just the opposite problem, because of the scarcity of rocks. Newcomers from the East often get so homesick for the sight of a stone that they import or dig up boulders, at considerable expense, and these are often displayed in the front yard or parking as curiosities. Such features are more appropriate in back yards. The common rock garden of the East, which is copied from the Alps via England, may be justifiable in a few Illinois back yards, but mountain flowers are hardly appropriate to prairie scenery, and the plants of cool, moist climates do not thrive in our hot, dry summers. A new type of rock garden aiming to fit our scenery and climate is being evolved. One step is the stratified rockwork in the Prairie River. (Circular 170, Fig. 106.) This had to be executed in tufa, the conventional material of the trade, as there was then no Illinois quarry where suitable stone could be had at a fair price in a region devoid of all stone. The next step is exemplified by Fig. 50, where the only plants used are the simple rock-loving flowers of the neighborhood instead of those exquisite gems from the alpine regions of the world which are dear to the hearts of all good rock-gardeners. Evi-

dently the owner regards quiet scenery as a more refined type of beauty than floral display, and such is the sober judgment of most authors of books on landscape gardening.

Lately a Wisconsin limestone has become popular in northern Illinois for stepping stones, ledges, dancing springs, cascades, and other naturalistic rockwork.

Restoration of the Dunes

THE reader probably fancies that dunes and sandy soil are of little interest or importance to Illinoisans. On the contrary, a large part of Chicago is so sandy that many thousand lot owners are having great trouble and expense in growing trees and shrubs, while the key to the whole problem is at the dunes, just beyond the state line, near Gary, Indiana. A popular complaint today in a large part of Chicago is "We can't grow anything in pure sand." After failure along conventional lines, a few members of the Prairie Club began to bring back from walks to the dunes some of the celebrated beauties of that region, among which are red cedar, juniper, witch hazel, june-berry, bittersweet, wafer ash, and sumac. To their surprise the dune materials throve wonderfully without good soil, fertilizers, or continual watering. Now the members of the Prairie Club are eagerly discussing "dune borders" and "dune gardens," and a strong sentiment has developed for buying the dune species from nurserymen instead of robbing the dunes.

51-52. Scene of a Restoration of Roadside Shrubbery by Illinois Farmers, and Wild Crab Apples Suggesting the Aim

"We farmers have sometimes saved trees along the roadside, but do trees alone give all the beauty we ought to have as a foil to the rich but monotonous farm land? Are not shrubs needed? Our neighbors think so.

"So we planted half a mile of highway in October, 1913, with crabs, haws, dogwoods, etc. This is the first piece of road designed and planted according to the 'Illinois way.'"—Harvey J. Sconce, Sidell, Vermilion county, Illinois.

"Unwittingly," says a former president of the club, "the members have hit upon the solution of the home-grounds question for the sandy parts of Illinois and the discovery may eventually save $500,000 to the citizens of Chicago, or more than it will cost them to buy the dunes and keep them forever for the people. About 100 kinds of these trees, shrubs, and perennials are suitable for home grounds and obtainable from nurserymen."

"Millions of dollars can eventually be saved," says one park designer, "by applying the lesson of the dunes to Illinois city parks. For example, the park boards commonly buy whole farms at $200 an acre or thereabouts in order to skim off the top soil and move it to the Chicago parks. Some of this expense may be necessary, because it is hard to maintain a good lawn on pure sand. Much of this effort, however, is a vain attempt to maintain fertility enough to grow foreign shrubs, and that is pouring money thru a sieve of sand, for the 'best sellers' of the nurseries are mostly of the swamp type, i. e., they have been adapted by nature to moist soil and cannot make long tap-roots like the drought-resisting species. To grow swamp plants in sand is to fight nature; to grow dune plants in sand is to harness nature. The highest type of beauty Chicago parks can ever have, in my opinion, is a dune restoration. Instead of leveling the sandhills and filling the valleys, why not run the drives thru the valleys, and plant the hills with sand-loving trees? Some day we shall have a Dune Park that will give Illinois international fame.

Home gardeners who have little space and money may apply the lesson of the dunes by planting some of the sand-loving materials enumerated on page 26, under Dry Soil.

Restoration of the Woods

THE following tale is perhaps one of the forty root-stories from which, according to Mark Twain, all jokes can be derived. A newly rich Chicagoan bought and built on the "North Shore" because of a piece of woods which he considered beautiful. "Why don't you get a landscape gardener?" his neighbors asked. "I will as soon as I clean up a little," he replied. So he cut out the shrubbery, and the landscape gardener made him put it all back at a cost of $2,000. He bought the same species from nurserymen and had to wait four or five years before he got as good an effect as the one he had destroyed. Every town in Illinois that has a wooded park generally has some variant of this story, because it is the regular thing for newly elected park boards to clean out the buck-brush, and then hire an expert who opens their eyes to the beauty of buck-brush and makes them plant it.

The first thing the landscape gardener makes the millionaire do to the old cow pasture is to fringe it with wild bushes, "so as to restore privacy and charm," as the expert says. (What he means is that woods do not amount to much if you can see right thru them; they are more interesting and beautiful if something is left to the imagination.) The next step is to restore the wild flowers, and the whole family soon catches the spirit of the thing. On their drives and walks they bring home plants and set them beside the trails, or gather seeds of wild flowers and sow them broadcast. One of the best restorations of this sort made by Illinois people is described in "Our Country Home," and "Our Country Life," by Frances Kinsley Hutchinson.

These simple methods of restoration can be used by Illinois farmers, especially when the woodlot is near the house. There may be no inducement for the farm renter to make any permanent improvements, but the average farm owner ought to care enough for his children's education in nature-lore and beauty to fence a portion of the woodlot, and let them restore the wild flowers that have been destroyed by cattle. Perhaps the first woodlot restoration made by a real farmer from a landscape gardener's design is the one made in 1915 at Sidell, by H. J. Sconce. See Figs. 37, 38. The farmers near Palestine, Illinois, also have a design for restoring shrubs and wild flowers to a piece of woodland in their country park. Henry Ford is making a woodland restoration of over 300 acres at Dearborn, Michigan. Eighty acres have already been thickly planted with trees and shrubs large enough to give in one year the effect of a forest thirty years old.

The city lot owner can, perhaps, ask his park board for a small woodland restoration, or vote for "outer park belts," and can apply the principle to his home grounds by making a "woodland border" in the shady corner.

Restoration of Roadside Beauty

MOST of the planting along the public roads of Illinois has been done by suburbanites or country gentlemen. In the wooded region north of Chicago it is not unusual to see shrubbery planted almost continuously in the parkings, or spaces between sidewalk and curb, especially in Winnetka and Highland Park, where all styles may be easily compared. Some of this has been inspired by Wildwood avenue in Graceland Cemetery. See Fig. 54. The pure spirit of restoration appears in Lake Forest, where E. L. Ryerson has planted haws, crabs, and plums, while on the prairie J. M. Cudahy has planted the same materials with red oak, hard maple, an undergrowth of common hazel, and such familiar prairie flowers as brown-eyed susan, butterfly weed, Aster laevis (the best blue aster), and the "Philadelphia lily."

One of the first restorations made on the prairie by a large owner of farm land is near Monticello, in Piatt county. This has changed the opinion of several influential farmers about roadside planting. Some are willing to plant trees along the roadside, but more prefer shrubs because they do less harm to crops. In the wooded parts of Illinois, a mile of roadside may be planted solidly with shrubs, but on the prairie, open spaces are necessary for breezeways and to give enough sun and air to keep the road in good condition. Incidentally, these open spaces greatly improve the prairie views, because they are enframed by planting. In this and other ways all the practical difficulties commonly made by farmers, engineers, and officials can be solved to the satisfaction of all classes of road-users on at least enough of the roadside to transform it from ugliness to beauty at a cost that property owners can afford.

Perhaps the first roadside planting done in the Illinois way is that described under Figs. 51, 52. Another leader is Spencer Otis, who has planted trees and shrubs on a mile near Barrington. Both cases are pure restorations, made by men who farm at a profit, in the open country, on rich corn land; and they are not on private drives, but on public roads.

The possibilities of roadside planting are enormous, for about two and one-half percent of the state's area is in roads, and if they are all planted, Illinois may have the largest state park system in the world—larger than the whole state of Rhode Island—without the cost of buying the land.

WE WILL

☐ Help our community to re-create in park, playground, cemetery, or roadside, one or more of these eight scenic units.

54. Or would you Like some of This Occasionally?
Some farmers can see beauty in ordinary "brush," even when the bushes are not in flower, and are willing to have trees along the roadside, trusting that the birds will keep the insects in check. (Wildwood avenue, Graceland Cemetery.) All trees and shrubs planted here are native.

53. Should Every Mile of Illinois Road be like This?
Some farmers believe that bare roads, decorated only with poles, wires, fences, and weeds have a depressing or deadening influence upon their families.

55-56.   Before and after Restoring the Prairie Feeling to a Park; the Broad View Conventionalized

"Here was a case of too much useless water and no chance for exercise. This shallow lake in Douglas Park had been made for show, and could not be used for canoeing or bathing. The neighborhood was densely settled and there was no place to play ball. Fortunately, there were two better lakes near by."

"So we developed those for use and beauty, and changed this to a ball field. We tried to restore the broad prairie view. It is conventionalized, for long grass would spoil a ball field. But we planted thousands of stratified Illinois shrubs. Anyone who skirts the field can get a suggestion of the prairie."—Jens Jensen.

VI—Can the Prairie be Restored?

BEFORE we can do any constructive think-ing about prairie scenery, we must define "prairie." By this we mean land that was treeless when the white man came to Illinois. It may be wild or cultivated, flat or rolling.

The first big fact to notice is that the sentimental appeal of the wild prairie is vastly greater than that of the cultivated prairie. A popular notion about the prairie is that its wonder and beauty have gone forever, and that there is nothing to do but mourn about it. Historians, travelers, novelists, poets, and musicians have tried to express the grandeur,

loneliness, and beauty of the wild prairie, but they rarely say a kind word for the beauty of cultivated prairie. And, apparently, it never occurs to them that any restoration of wild prairie is possible. The one overwhelming impression that all travelers got from the wild prairie was the infinite extent of it. Nowadays people do not see how the idea of infinity can be brought home with the old-time power without the use of a tract of land so large that no individual can afford to pay taxes on it and let it lie idle. To re-create a big, wild prairie is a state-park proposition.

Wanted—a Prairie Park

"SOME day," says one far-seeing citizen, "every middle-western state will make one prairie reservation before it is too late or re-create one wild prairie for the people to enjoy forever. It would take less land than is popularly supposed. For the main purpose is to get out of sight of trees and away from every suggestion of man's work. This can perhaps be done on 1,000 acres, if the land rolls enough. A dozen parties could then be in as many different valleys, yet each could enjoy without interruption for short periods

57.   The Broad View of the Prairie, Framed by Stratified Honey Locust

For constructive purposes all prairie scenery may be reduced to two units—the broad view and the long view. The broad view is the one that suggests in-finite extent, and is the more inspiring for occasional visits. See Fig. 58.

the apparent infinity of green grass and blue sky which impressed the pioneers as powerfully as the ocean. For contrast, the big open space could be skirted by the other great element of Illinois scenery—the irregular border of woodland, which originally defined the typical Illinois prairie, with its pleasant suggestion of a river hidden within the forest. Such a prairie park seems necessary to "recharge the batteries" of those who do the world's work. The millions who toil in great cities ordinarily have but two weeks' vacation. Several states now provide a chance to camp in the wilds at the least expense. Possibly prairie schooners could be used. The educational value of the park would be increased by combining with it an arboretum or botanical garden large enough to teach the people the names of the most interesting trees and wild flowers which they find in the adjacent woodland and prairie. I believe this dream can be realized at a cost which many a private citizen can afford as a gift to the people. Universities and libraries are doubtless more important to humanity, but a prairie park might touch a very responsive chord in the popular heart and ought to win the everlasting gratitude of mankind."

Miniature Prairies

CAN a bit of wild prairie be restored for the sake of beauty, even if it lacks the suggestion of infinity? Certainly. Occasionally, one hears of some old settler who, in some waste corner of the farm, saved a bit of prairie sod to remind him of old times. Or a plainsman, like Bishop Quayle's father, willed that his last resting place should be beneath a strip of Buffalo grass, and enjoined his son to see that the wild grass is never run out by the domesticated. One may respect such sentiments, but the results can hardly be called beautiful. The beauty of the wild prairie can be restored in an impressive way to one park in every Illinois city by means of a "miniature prairie" of the kind described by William Trelease.

"I wish a plan for a ten-acre prairie restoration, surrounded by trees and shrubbery, in the borders of which perennial flowers may be grown in beds for botanical students. The center is to be thickly planted with bluestem and other wild grasses, amid which the characteristic prairie flowers, like sunflowers, gaillardia, compass plant, and blazing star, are to fight for existence. How long it will take to restore anything like the thick sod of the wild prairie, no one knows. But in two or three years there should be a strong suggestion of prairie wildness, because the flowers will seem to float on a sea of grasses. This effect can hardly be produced in the ordinary hardy border, but it seems practical in any city park that can afford from two to five acres or more for such a feature."

Prairie Gardens and Prairie Borders

ILLINOISANS are now experimenting with "prairie gardens" of many kinds. The most promising type is a protest against the conventional shrubbery border which has become effeminate thru over-refinement. In order to carry the eye easily from trees to lawn and vice versa, the gardener often makes many gradations. First, he puts a row of tall shrubs, next a row of medium bushes, then low shrubs, and finally a continuous edging of perennial flowers, which may be similarly graduated. In seeking for a more virile kind of border the leader of the prairie school went for inspiration to the place where wood and prairie meet. "There," he says, "I found the strongest and most satisfactory border that nature has ever given man, so far as my observations go. The full-grown border of haws and crabs has been likened by some to mosaic, by others to lace work, while some declare it is a tone poem. By comparison the conventional shrubbery border, full of gaudy

'best sellers,' seems a kaleidoscope or crazy quilt. Stand off and view the ordinary border of shrubs, and you will see how poor a job it makes of uniting lawn and woods. It needs small trees to bind together forest and meadow. The bold leap that nature often makes from haws and crabs down to the prairie flowers reminds me of some powerful and beautiful animal, slipping silently from forest shade into a sea of grasses. Therefore, in my new prairie gardens I make no transition between small trees and lawn, except that I have extra-wide, irregular colonies of phlox, using the wild phlox, or a variety with flattish clusters, like Rynstrom."

Those who find the preceding paragraph too poetic may at least have a practical border of prairie flowers —say 3x25 feet, choosing from Nos. 1 to 21, and 88 to 106, on page 24. Every Illinois city should have in at least one park a "prairie border"— with the grasses, composites, and other flowers labeled. It will not be like the prairie, but it will serve to teach the rising generation about the famous prairie flowers of which they read in novels and histories.

The Scenic Value of Cultivated Prairie

SO much for the wild prairie and its restoration. As to cultivated prairie, travelers generally admit that the feeling of infinity can still be had from the high spots, and they also admit that a sea of corn is beautiful. Easterners commonly acknowledge that rolling prairie is full of inspiration, but they usually say that flat prairie is not attractive. Foreign eyes are not educated to see the slight undulations in "flat" prairie that give so much quiet enjoyment every day to those who live on the land. Many plain farmers feel this beauty so deeply that they do not like to talk about it, but is repression the best attitude? Can we take any honest pride in prairie beauty if we never spend an hour or a dollar to save any of it? Is it not better to discuss and practice restoration?

Whether the prairie is a higher order of beauty than that of mountainous country we leave to popular disputation. Those who have been reared amid one type often feel uneasy in the other. But it is not safe to tell an Illinois man that flat land is unattractive and has no possibility of making one of the most beautiful regions of the world. One resident of Lake Forest is reported to have said, "The beauty of ordinary, flat, cultivated prairie is so clear to me that I was one of the first to turn away from the more obvious beauty of Lake Michigan and the wooded ravines to build on the prairie, where I run a farm that aims to make money. To unsympathetic eastern eyes our prairie view may look tame and new, but we would rather have it, even if we must wait for the trees."

58. The Long View of the Prairie

The long, narrow glimpses are more human and intimate than the broad views, like Fig. 57. The small picture above and to the left is framed by cottonwood.

Restoring the Broad View

FOR constructive purposes all prairie scenery may here be reduced to two units, the broad view and the long view. See Figs. 57, 58. The broad view is the one that suggests infinity and power, and is the more in-

59. Long View of Prairie Conventionalized

"Instead of putting a single row of trees down the center of this parking," says the designer, "I left the center open and put native shrubbery at the sides to suggest the long view of the prairie or the farm lane at its best." See page 18.

spiring for occasional visits; the long view is more human and intimate, and often more satisfactory to live with.

One of the first attempts to restore the broad view is the playground in Garfield Park. See Figs. 55, 56. Another may be summarized as follows: "I have a ten-acre pasture on which I am trying to restore as much of the wild-prairie beauty as the average farmer can afford—and no more, for I am much opposed to display. I am not prepared to advocate surrounding every field with a solid border of shrubbery, altho some authorities believe that such borders will keep down insects by attracting birds. But I do believe that the average Illinois farmer can enrich his family life greatly by bordering one field near the house with native shrubs. The financial loss is more than offset by the pleasure of seeing the flowers, berries, and birds, and above all by the chance to idealize his broad view. For example, we built in the open because we prefer farm life to lake and woods, but the ordinary broad view on Illinois farms is certainly commonplace for a good part of the year. To idealize it we have planted several elms near the door to enframe the prairie, and one big one near the middle of the pasture to suggest the solitary giants that occasionally enlivened the wild prairie. At the edge of the pasture are planted some hard maples and other trees to remind us of the distant woodlands which formerly bounded the typical prairie view in Illinois. The shrubbery surrounding the pasture consists of common wild crabs, plums, haws, sumac, hazel, sheepberry, chokecherry, witch hazel, smooth rose, etc., which will idealize the flat prairie by restoring some of the wild beauty. For this reason I would much rather have these native shrubs than miles of Japanese barberry hedges, or the showier beauty of foreign spireas, hydrangeas, and crimson ramblers, which seem to me quite out of harmony with Illinois farm scenery."

What else can the farmer do with a broad view? Luckily he does not have to own all the land and keep it idle. The important thing is to control the high place. Sometimes he may build on it, sometimes locate a drive along the top of a ridge, sometimes put a seat at the best spot. Often he can enframe the best view by pairs of trees in front of the house, beside the dining room, or along the road, as has been done near Sidell and Barrington.

Restoring the Long View

BY "long view" is meant the narrow opening between farmsteads and woodlots which often extends for several miles. See Fig. 58. It does not need to go off to infinity. Indeed, many persons prefer to have it stopped by a hazy ridge or misty piece of woods. They believe that a finite view is easier to understand and love than an infinite one. The long view is the home-like and friendly side of the prairie. Farmers have noticed the long view less, but when their attention is called to it they are often quick to see its practical advantages. For a person can often frame a long view from a home window at less cost and in less time than a broad view.

One of the most inspiring long views in America was made by Mr. Simonds in Graceland Cemetery. See Fig. 60. The famous English authority, William Robinson, greatly admired this vista. It lies within a city of two million inhabitants, yet it occupies only about 10x400 feet, or say one-tenth of an acre. One critic has called Fig. 60 "the straight way to the great hope," because it points to Nature's annual resurrection as a seeming promise of the resurrection of the soul. The next picture (Fig. 61) he calls "the straight way to bad taste," because it shows one of the many ways in which fine artworks are desecrated by a display of wealth. Can we not have in every Illinois community one cemetery of the highest type?

The farmer has a fine chance to idealize the long view. "I never frame a long prairie view with spectacular trees, like Lombardy poplar, as the eastern men do," says an Illinois landscape gardener. "Even red cedars do not look right on the Illinois farm. Nature left the exclamation point out of the prairie scenery. The kind of accent she made for the prairie is not vertical, but horizontal. Let the farmer frame his long view with a pair of vase-formed elms or cottonwoods." See Fig. 58.

In the city the long view of the prairie can be symbolized. For example, Graceland Cemetery was not consciously modeled on the prairie, but Fig. 60 suggests how it can be done in a park or cemetery on 4,000 square feet.

Has the long prairie view been conventionalized? "Yes," says one Illinois landscape gardener, "I deliberately aimed at this on Logan boulevard, Chicago, along the half-mile between Milwaukee and California avenues, and also on Humboldt boulevard. See Fig. 59. Formerly gardeners used to put a line of tall trees at uniform distances thru the middle of a parkway, or scatter shrubs for show. Nowadays, to prevent holdups and disorderly conduct, it is necessary to keep the center open, light it, and avoid all places of concealment, such as pockets of shrubbery. These conditions give a fine chance to conventionalize the long view of the prairie by planting at either side of the parking haws, crabs, and gray dogwood, which becomes stratified when old. Of course, in all conventional work, Nature's original suggestion must be hidden from the crowd, or it will be misunderstood and ridiculed. But the discerning few who look down the center of the parking will feel the long view of the prairie."

Methods of Restoration

NO methods absolutely new to the art of landscape gardening are practiced by restorers, but in the most elaborate restorations, four sciences are pursued farther than usual along the lines indicated below. Some investigation is necessary or the product cannot be called a restoration.

1. *Systematic botany.* The first step is to make a botanical survey, or list of all plant materials now growing wild on the property, or at least the most important ones. Since some desirable species are missing, the next step is to consult a county flora to find whether they grew in the vicinity originally and whether they were common and characteristic or rare and untypical. Unfortunately there is no state flora, but see page 27.

2. *State and local history.* The main types of scenery in nearly all parts of the state have been described at length by travelers or pioneers. For samples see page 27. The county courthouse should be searched for the oldest records, especially the original survey, which sometimes names and locates the finest trees that served as landmarks.

3. *Ecology.* This is a new and fascinating branch of botany that deals with plant societies. It gives combinations of plants that are far more effective in restorations than any which can be invented by man, because Nature has evolved them by ages of experiment. As an introduction to this science, see books listed on page 27.

4. *Ornithology.* Restoration of the birds should be an organic part of every scheme for reproducing Illinois scenery or vegetation. The means of attracting birds are described in an immense number of bulletins and catalogs. A letter to the U. S. Department of Agriculture or to the National Association of Audubon Societies, 1974 Broadway, New York, will put one in touch.

WE WILL

☐ Restore some feeling of the prairie to our home grounds by having an open, central lawn flanked by some stratified bushes and prairie wild flowers.

☐ Have a prairie garden, miniature prairie, or prairie border.

☐ Help Illinois create a prairie park as described on pages 16, 17.

☐ Ask our park board to frame a prairie view, like Figs. 57 to 59.

☐ Help our community secure or restore a bit of wild prairie.

60. "The Straight Way to the Great Hope"
This vista has been so called because it points to Nature's annual resurrection as a seeming promise of the resurrection of the soul. See under "Restoring the Long View."

61. "The Straight Way to Bad Taste"
Desecration of an artwork by display of wealth. Can we not have one landscape cemetery with high ideals in every Illinois community? See above.

62. Repetition of the Prairie Line on a Golf Green by Cutting Out Border Trees Less Valuable Than Haws
The golf club at Winnetka tired of hard, straight lines thru the woods, so they employed Mr. Simonds to secure more natural vistas.

VII—Everyone Can Apply the Principle of Repetition

HOW THE "PRAIRIE SPIRIT" HAS BEEN BROUGHT INTO THE DAILY LIVES OF RICH AND POOR, IN CITY, SUBURBS, AND COUNTRY, IN ALL PARTS OF THE PRAIRIE STATE

ANYONE can discover the magical part played by repetition in the Illinois landscape simply by walking or driving to the nearest high spot that commands a broad view of the prairie. How eagerly does the stranger look forward to his first glimpse of the prairie and what an unforgetable experience it is! The first thing that strikes everyone is the bigness of it, for it seems infinite, as the ocean does. But as your glance instinctively follows the gentle, wave-like roll of the land, it comes to the place where land and sky meet and there it stops. See Fig. 57. The prairie horizon has been called "the strongest line in the western hemisphere." You may try to look at something else, but your eyes will keep coming back to the horizon until you follow it around the circle. No wider view is possible on earth, when you can see all the land-circle and half of the sky-circle simply by turning on your heel. To get an experience like this people often climb high mountains, sometimes with danger, always with difficulty and expense. But the Illinois farmer can get his broad view with little effort and no expense, simply by mounting a land-wave twelve or fifteen feet high. Do we Illinoisans appreciate our privileges and enjoy to the ut-

most the inspirational value of these high places? If not, we are lucky when our memory is jogged by some traveler who says he has come 5,000 miles just to see the prairie; that Europe has nothing like it; and that the prairie is the most characteristic scenery on the American continent. But, however we Illinoisans may differ in our appreciation of scenery, we generally agree that the greatest prairie view is the one that enables you to follow the line of the horizon "clear round the world."

After discovering the overwhelming importance of the horizontal line comes the second revelation. You notice an absence of spectacular forms; there are no steep hills, pointed rocks, or spiry trees; all vertical lines are obscured. At first you are a little disappointed, because you are used to picturesque or romantic scenery, and here is something very different. Then your curiosity is aroused as to what can be the secret of the prairie's beauty. For the prairie is obviously beautiful, but its beauty is hard to define. You begin to study the main features of the scenery and find that there are usually five—land, sky, woods, crops, and water. Next you notice that the distant woodlands have level or gently

rounded tops; that the corn crop is level, as well as the ground; and if there be a lake or river, that, too, is level. If the prairie looks its best there will be fleecy clouds in the sky, sailing toward the horizon like fleets of flat-bottomed ships. Then it gradually dawns upon you that the essence of the prairie's beauty lies in all these horizontal lines, no two of which are of the same length or at the same elevation, but all of which repeat in soft and gentle ways the great story of the horizon.

Thus, you have learned straight from nature the great law of repetition, the importance of which can be quickly verified when you get back to your library. For Ruskin, in his "Elements of Drawing," explains that repetition is one of the nine laws of composition that are fundamental to all the fine arts. After describing the law of principality (by which he means making one feature more important than all the rest), he says, "Another important means of expressing unity is to mark some kind of sympathy among the different objects, and perhaps the pleasantest, because most surprising, kind of sympathy is when one group imitates or repeats another; not in the way of balance or symmetry, but subordinately, like a faraway and broken echo of it."

63-64. Before and after Repeating the Prairie on the Parking of a City Street
"The people of Highland Park planted about $700 worth of Illinois shrubs in public places in 1914. Our environment is woodland and therefore many of us believe in planting the parkings in order to intensify the sylvan charm of the town and connect all private places with the town ideal. But woodland beauty needs a foil, so we have some open spaces and many haws and crabs to suggest the great prairie beyond us."—Everett L. Millard, Highland Park, Illinois.

65. Repetition of Horizon and Whitecaps by Elders

The horizon is, perhaps, the strongest line in the prairie states. It can be beautifully repeated on the prairie or beside the lake by planting trees and shrubs with horizontal branches or flower clusters. For E. L. Millard's explanation, see page 12, column 2.

66. Repetition of Prairie by Stratified Haws in Summer

Hawthorns are still abundant along many roads in Illinois and are much admired for their deep, mysterious shadows, their flat flower clusters, red fruits, autumn colors, and the stratified branching of some species, which is most obvious in winter. They help to restore the song birds.

How far nature has carried the principle of repetition in Illinois you can easily discover on your next long drive to the country, unless you are so unfortunate as to live in one of those sections where nearly all native vegetation has been swept away by men whose souls have not yet been opened to the refining influences of beauty. In the latter case you may get some light by analyzing the list of materials on pages 24, 25. Of the 200 species of Illinois materials listed, eighty-seven are stratified in branch or flower. This is about forty-three percent, or, say, two-fifths of the native species that are in cultivation.

Has your discovery any practical value to every Illinois citizen? Certainly, provided refining influences of any kind are worth while. Of course, if life is only for dollars, we should steel our hearts against any softening influences. But if we believe in home and children and the higher life, it will be an immense help to have beautiful home grounds. Your discovery means that you can reproduce some of the effects illustrated on pages 19 to 23. It means that no two places in Illinois need look just alike, for everyone can make a different combination of the stratified materials enumerated on page 24. It means that all places can be part of one great scheme to make Illinois beautiful. It means that we Illinoisans need try no longer to imitate the East, which can always excel us in evergreens, especially rhododendrons and mountain laurel. For we have discovered a type of beauty in which the prairie states naturally excel. By working out the principle of repetition in all sorts of ways we can restore and intensify a type of beauty which mountainous, hilly, and arid regions cannot duplicate.

The full beauty of your discovery comes only when you have committed yourself to it by planting on your home grounds a considerable quantity of stratified material. Then every day brings some fresh revelation of the law of repetition. You see it in every house and statue that you admire, and hear it in every piece of music. You begin to search for the subtler forms of it in poetry, painting, and the drama. Every book you pick up seems to have some bearing on it, and if you are tempted to exaggerate its importance Ruskin restores your perspective by telling the other laws of composition, viz., principality, continuity, curvature, radiation, contrast, interchange, consistency, and harmony. All these laws are merely devices for securing unity, and the supreme pleasure connected with repetition comes when we ask, "What is the unity that underlies prairie scenery?"

When you stand upon a high place overlooking the prairie, what seems to you its deepest meaning? Some say the dominant note is peacefulness—that this middle-western country will never be invaded by a foreign foe, and the landscape expresses this sense of security. Others declare that it is an expression of God's bounty. The horizon is but a symbol of a religious idea which each person may express in his own way, just as everyone may make his own interpretation of a piece of music. Every great style in art, it is said, is based upon some religious idea. The

67. Horizontal Branches of Swamp White Oak

This circular bed of foreign flowers may be allowable in this case, but it belongs to the gardenesque style. The prairie spirit suggests American bluebells or Canada lily fringing the shrubbery. (Graceland.)

68. Repetition of Water Line by Tupelo

The tupelo or pepperidge is famed for its early red autumn color, and is even more valued for its stratification, which is probably the strongest among deciduous trees. (Graceland.)

69. At Wood-Edges Nature Suggests Prairie

"I would have planted composite flowers here to repeat the prairie, but nature restores them abundantly in the form of brown-eyed susans and asters." —A resident of Ravinia, Illinois.

70. A Subtle Case of Repetition—American Hornbeam

This small tree has slender branches, which are conspicuously horizontal only in winter, especially after rain, snow, or an ice storm. (Carpinus.)

71. Some Repeat the Horizontal Only When in Flower

Above is a thorn (Crataegus mollis) which does not have horizontal branches. The same is true of the viburnums, elders, and most shrubby dogwoods.

soul of Gothic architecture is its symbol of aspiration—the spire, which the pointed arch repeats in outline, while both forms can be reduced to a single line, the vertical. This line is repeated by the spiry evergreen trees of Europe. The ascending line characterizes the Chinese temple, and is repeated by many of the Chinese evergreens. The horizontal line characterizes the prairie style of architecture and landscape gardening, and this line is repeated by stratified hawthorns and crab apples.

The necessity of softening a dominant line by repetition is illustrated by the awe-inspiring loneliness of the wild prairie. Pioneers and travelers were at times afraid to be alone with such an infinite thing, as their records testify. Perhaps the frankest utterance of the old attitude occurs in a French traveler's account of the Russian steppes. Speaking of the eternal sameness among the people, in dress, speech, and houses, he attempts to explain their melancholy by the endless breadth of the land, and ends by exclaiming, "It is impossible to live with the Infinite and be happy." Is there any minister today who would agree to such an assertion, especially the author of "The Great Companion?" Does not every religion today emphasize love of the Infinite, rather than fear? And is not the prairie less fearful and more lovable since its sea of hissing grasses has changed to fields of corn? The

modified prairie may be less beautiful now than the wild prairie, but it is pleasanter to live with, and it may become one of the most beautiful regions in the world if we take on a missionary zeal for building houses and gardens that repeat the prairie line. For repetition translates the fearful Infinite into the friendly finite. Our stratified materials break up the horizon into bits that we can grasp and understand. They will enable Illinois to idealize the scenery of an entire state.

So, every Illinois citizen, no matter what his religion, can express the modern, intimate, and joyful relation with the Infinite by planting some stratified trees or bushes that symbolize the great horizon which in turn is but a symbol of the great reality that underlies all religions. Symbolism always has been and ever will be natural and necessary to mankind. We need something to express the infinite peace, plenty, and happiness of the prairie country. What better symbol can we have on the lawn than the stratified hawthorn, loaded in the spring with flowers and in the autumn filled with brilliant red fruits on which the birds feast? In the flower garden the first aim, of course, is flowers or color, but there may be a deeper, hidden meaning also. Gaillardias may stand for the prairie spirit and larkspurs for the Gothic. The aspiring and the stratified flowers may be regarded as religious symbols.

Each is a good foil for the other. (Fig. 73.)

Granting that repetition is an important principle, can it not be overdone or poorly done? Certainly. It is conceivable that some sentimentalist might plant only stratified material and make a mess of it, but there are too many other attractive plants to make this a serious matter. A joke may stand only one repetition, but the prairie's story will bear retelling many times. And the stratified materials of Illinois are never loud or coarse storytellers. The danger of overplanting them is practically nothing compared with the universal tendency to overdo the formal and gardenesque styles. Nature often suggests symmetry, but never pushes it to the extreme of a formal garden, in which everything is balanced. The prairie furnishes haws and crabs to accentuate her idea, but they are moderate and peaceful compared with the gardenesque style, which kills peace in home grounds because it is all accent and that of the flashiest kind, like cannas and coleus. Put your trust in the prairie. The danger of overdoing her type of beauty is remote.

WE WILL

☐ Repeat the strongest line in the prairie states by planting some of the stratified materials enumerated on page 24.

72. The Prairie Spirit in the Shady Corner

The most beautiful repeater of the prairie among woodland flowers is wild blue phlox (Phlox divaricata), here planted under shrubs at Graceland.

73. The Prairie Spirit in the Sunny Garden

The first aim in a flower garden or hardy border is flowers and color, but there may also be a deeper, hidden meaning, as explained above.

74-75. The First Principle in Adapting the Prairie Style is to Intensify each Peculiar Type of Scenery

Looking down from this bridge the ravine seems very deep, when measured by this wild grape, which has climbed from the bottom up a tall tree. E. L. Millard, Highland Park, Illinois.

Among the strongest features of woodland are the arbors of wild grape. They furnish shade, protection from rain, food for the birds, and beauty. The vines are rampant and often need restraint. Glencoe, Illinois.

VIII—Adapting the Prairie Style to Other Kinds of Scenery

HOW TO INTENSIFY THE PECULIAR BEAUTY OF EACH TYPE AND HOW TO BLEND ALL IN ONE GREAT SCHEME FOR BEAUTIFYING ILLINOIS

THOSE Illinoisans who live amid scenery that is different from the prairie will naturally ask, "Is the prairie style only for the prairie, or can it be adapted to our conditions?" The answer is that it has already been adapted to all types of Illinois scenery and by methods that can be easily illustrated.

For example, consider the wooded parts of Illinois, which comprise about fifteen to eighteen percent of the state's area, and are very attractive to home-builders. Do you think the "prairie house" shown in Fig. 76 fits the woodland? Evidently the architect did not try to make his house as conspicuous as possible —quite the opposite—for he has put the house not outside the woods but inside, and taken great pains to save the trees closest the house. For the same reason he has made the house long and low, instead of tall and narrow. Also he has used more wood and less stucco than for a house in the open. Finally he has stained the siding brown and the roof green to harmonize with tree trunks and foliage. The landscape gardener can carry the

adaptation one degree farther by planting near the house those shrubs that are so dependent upon woodland shade that they rarely thrive without it, for example, red elder, maple-leaved arrow-wood, and round-leaved dogwood. We now perceive that in woodland, and in all other kinds of Illinois scenery, adaptation consists largely in intensifying the peculiarities of each scenic type.

How to Intensify Each Scenic Type

IF you build on the lake bluffs you will naturally plant red cedar, Canadian juniper, white pine, red oak, gray poplar, hop hornbeam, Buffalo berry, red-twigged dogwood, Aster laevis, and wild grape. (Fig. 74.)

If your garden is a ravine you will naturally plant the great specialties of the ravines, namely, American linden, sugar maple, witch hazel, hepatica, bloodroot, meadow rue, trillium, and wild grape. See Fig. 75.

If you are so fortunate as to own a bit of river bottom, you will naturally plant more of the wonderful trees that reach their great-

est development on the flood plain, namely, American elm, buttonball, cottonwood, ash, walnut, butternut, tulip tree, hackberry, coffee tree, mulberry, redbud, and buckeye. Other plants that intensify the feeling of nearness to a river are the riverbank grape, wild gooseberry, American bluebell, wild blue phlox, western adder's tongue (Erythronium albidum), Jacob's ladder, and Collinsia verna.

If you live on drained land that was formerly a swamp or bog, you may be able to grow some of the finest products of that scenic type, namely, the bur, scarlet, and swamp white oaks, red maple, arborvitae, American larch, Nyssa sylvatica (Fig. 68), winterberry, red and black chokeberry, flowering currant, buttonbush, wintergreen, Rubus hispidus, cinnamon fern, royal fern, and marsh marigold.

If you live on a sandhill or dune, you can make it a beauty spot instead of a desert by planting the white pines (Fig. 77), gray pine, red cedar, bur oak, frost grape (Vitis cordifolia), chokecherry, and sand cherry.

If you live on a clay hill you may have

76. How "Prairie Architecture" has been Adapted to Woodland

House put inside the woods—not outside; trees nearest house carefully saved; house made long and low; woodwork painted brown like tree trunks, and roof green, like foliage. Needs shrubbery at foundation to connect house, woods, and prairie. (Frank Lloyd Wright, architect.)

77. White Pine is Adapted to Dunes, Bluffs, and Rocks

It also connects these types with the prairie by repeating the horizon. Longer-lived than the Scotch or Austrian pine, and looks more at home about the farmstead or at edge of woodlot. Must have drainage. Thrives better on rolling prairie than on flat land.

78-79. The Second Principle in Adapting the Prairie Style—Connect the Other Types of Scenery with the Prairie

June-berry, when old, becomes stratified, thus giving the suggestion of prairie which nature has put into the heart of every type of Illinois scenery.

The rounded tops of haws repeat the rolling land, while the species with stratified branches suggest the level prairie. "The haws are the most significant feature in our landscape."—Mrs. Lew Wallace, Gale Farm, Galesburg, Illinois.

the good fortune to preserve the original white and red oak, shell-bark hickory, sugar maple, and even the beech. If the undergrowth has been destroyed, the proper companions for the above are the dotted and scarlet haws, hazel, viburnums, yellow violet, and wood anemone.

If you live on a rocky hill you may accentuate its original picturesqueness by planting the dwarf rose (Rosa humilis), ninebark, chokeberry, staghorn sumac, and wafer ash.

If you own a bit of pond you can make a water garden containing water lily and perhaps American lotus, wild rice, pickerel weed, arrowhead, bur reed, and cat-tail.

It will be hard for man to improve on the above combinations, for they have been adapted to these scenic units thru ages of experimentation by nature. All of them are genuine Illinois examples and are reported by Henry C. Cowles in "The Plant Societies of Chicago and Vicinity."

Now, if the essence of adaptation in landscape gardening is intensification of the native flora instead of importing foreign beauty, it is obvious that the most important methods must be conservation and restoration. But these are about two-thirds of the prairie style. Therefore, the prairie style can, to this extent at least, be adapted to all parts of Illinois. In fact, it has been, as shown by Figs. 41 to 48.

How to Blend All Types of Scenery

BUT this is not all of the story, for if each scenic type were emphasized to the utmost and nothing done to connect one type with another, the contrasts would be too strong. Now comes to our assistance the law of interchange, which is explained by Ruskin as follows: "Closely connected with the law of contrast is a law which enforces the unity of opposite things, by giving to each a portion of the character of the other. * * * The typical purpose of the law of interchange is, of course, to teach us how opposite natures may be helped and strengthened by receiving each, as far as they can, some impress, or imparted power, from the other."

Let us now apply the principle of interchange to those who live amid woodland. For example, the house in Fig. 76 is not wholly of the woods, like a log cabin; it has a decided suggestion of the sunny prairie outside, owing to its style of design. Only one more touch is needed to unite the home grounds with the outside world, viz., a group of the round-leaved dogwood next to the house. For this species (Cornus circinata) clearly unites in itself two opposite types of scenery. It belongs to the woods, because it will not thrive in full sunshine, and yet its horizontal branches clearly suggest the pleasant prairie outside. Other plants that can

be used to connect woods and prairie are maple-leaved arrow-wood, witch hazel, and wild blue phlox. The two last named will grow in full sun as well as shade.

One of the most delightful themes for a walk in the country is to discover how far nature has worked out this law of interchange. At the edge of every minor type of scenery she has generally interwoven some plants that suggest the dominant type of Illinois scenery—the prairie. She has even carried the prairie spirit into the heart of the most contrasting scenery by means of stratified plants. For example, at the edge of a clearing, nature restores the brown-eyed susans and other composite flowers, as explained under Fig. 69, while in the inmost recesses of the woods she expresses the prairie spirit by red elder, maidenhair fern, meadow rue, wild spikenard (Aralia racemosa), wood aster, and wild blue phlox (Fig. 72). At Starved Rock her crowning feature is the dramatic group of white pines, thru whose stratified branches she shows you the stratified rock, while both features grandly echo the noble valley of the Illinois and the distant prairie. At the dunes near Chicago she brings another type of wild beauty to the climax shown in Fig. 77, where white pine repeats the strongest line in the Middle West. At the waterside she will teach you the prairie spirit thru tupelo (Fig. 68), swamp white oak (Fig. 67), red-twigged dogwood, blue ash, and in favored localities, thru red maple and red elder. In the exclusive precincts of the ravines she will gently suggest the democracy of the prairie thru witch hazel, round-leaved dogwood, meadow rue, spikenard, sarsaparilla, maidenhair, Aster laevis, and even by the june-berry, which becomes stratified when old, as shown in Fig. 78. But on the aristocratic bluffs poor Nature may be forced to trepan the obstinate skull and insert the prairie idea thru white pine (as she clearly does at White Pine Grove in Ogle county and at Sinnissippi Farm near Oregon, Illinois), or else by elder as in Fig. 65.

Has nature put stratified material into every kind of scenery in the world and can the prairie style be adapted to every country? No. The prairie style ought not to be copied by people who live among the mountains or in the arid regions, simply because their friends in Illinois may have something beautiful in that style. The essence of landscape gardening is the accentuation of native scenery, and the strong feature in mountainous countries is the vertical line, which mountaineers should repeat by planting their own aspiring evergreens, such as white spruce, hemlock, and balsam. We can hardly forbid them making some slight suggestion of the neigh-

boring plain. Indeed, there are enough stratified materials in the mountains to give the hint. But in no type of scenery that differs from the prairie should people plant more stratified than unstratified materials. The law of principality requires that one thing shall be dominant, and on the prairie stratified plants should probably be more in evidence than anywhere else in the world. The law of contrast shows how the true character of a dominant idea can be brought out by contrast, provided the opposing idea is subservient. Therefore, on the prairie it is right to plant a few reminders of the woods and waterside. Conversely, if you live amid different scenery from the prairie, emphasize that difference all you can, but do not forget to have some suggestion of the prairie also.

Is there any other way by which all types of Illinois scenery and all home grounds can be blended in one great scheme for beautifying the state? Obviously, we could plant our state tree, which is simply called the "native oak." (The "Act in Relation to a State Tree and a State Flower," approved February 21, 1908, appears as Chapter 57A, Sec. 16, on page 1320 of Hurd's Revised Statutes of 1913.) We are richer in oaks than in any other kind of trees, since we have eighteen species, but the most characteristic of all is the bur or mossy-cup oak, which is as rugged in appearance as Lincoln. It should be planted in every part of Illinois where it is likely to thrive. Unfortunately the state flower will not help us much, for by "prairie violet" people commonly mean the large-flowered, long-stemmed Viola cucullata, which is not peculiar to the prairie, being common in the woods and in the East. Moreover, this violet is disappointing in cultivation, making its response to rich soil by producing more leaves than flowers. Of all the plants popularly named after the prairie, the prairie rose is the most satisfactory for general cultivation thruout the state. And since Illinois is the Prairie State, we may be justified in calling it the Illinois rose, and making it a symbol of the "Illinois way of planting." But to symbolize the prairie style that is to fit the Middle West, shall we not choose that quintessence of the prairie spirit—the hawthorn?

WE WILL

☐ Intensify the peculiar scenery amid which we live by planting strong masses of the materials native to our type.

☐ Plant a few stratified materials to remind us of the bountiful prairie on which the prosperity of Illinois largely depends, and to show others that we wish to cooperate with any scheme for beautifying Illinois.

IX—Materials Used in the Prairie Style

PERMANENT ORNAMENTAL PLANTS NATIVE TO ILLINOIS WHICH CAN BE OBTAINED FROM NURSERYMEN

THIS list is not complete, but it contains nearly all native plants that are advisable for small places, as well as a good many that are suitable only for parks and large estates. It is impractical to give full descriptions of all the plants mentioned, and the garden-lover must look to horticultural publications, nursery catalogs, and local authorities for detailed information.

Nurserymen. Most good nurserymen offer some of the species mentioned in this circular. Those named below offer a considerable variety of trees, shrubs, and perennials native to Illinois. Augustine Nursery Co., Normal, Ill.; Geo. Wm. Bassett, Hammonton, N. J.; Biltmore Nursery Co., Biltmore, N. C.; H. A. Dreer, 714 Chestnut St., Philadelphia; Edward Gillett, Southwick, Mass.; F. H.

Horsford, Charlotte, Vt.; Harlan P. Kelsey, Salem, Mass.; Klehm's Nurseries, Arlington Heights, Ill.; Henry Kohankie and Son, Painesville, Ohio; Leesley Bros., N. Crawford and Peterson Aves., Chicago; Naperville Nurseries, Naperville, Ill.; Swain Nelson and Sons Co., Marquette Bldg., Chicago; Peterson Nursery, 30 N. LaSalle St., Chicago; the Storrs and Harrison Co., Painesville, Ohio.

Class I. Stratified Materials or Symbols of the Prairie (All native to Illinois)

(The practical uses to which these are best suited are indicated in the article on page 26. Incidentally they may symbolize or idealize prairie scenery or Illinois surroundings. Those marked * have strong horizontal branches; the others have flat flower clusters.)

GROUP 1. PERENNIALS AND NEAR PERENNIALS.

a. For garden cultivation in full sun.
1. Asclepias tuberosa. Butterfly weed.
2. Aster lævis. Smooth aster.
3. Boltonia asteroides. Aster-like boltonia.
4. Coreopsis lanceolata. Lance-leaved tickseed.
5. Coreopsis tinctoria (*Calliopsis elegans*). Golden coreopsis. (Annual, but self-sows.)
6. Echinacea purpurea (*Rudbeckia purpurea*). Purple coneflower.
7. Eupatorium cœlestinum (*Conoclinium coelestinum*). Mist flower.
8. Euphorbia corollata. Flowering spurge.
9. Gaillardia aristata (*G. grandiflora*). Perennial gaillardia. See Fig. 73.
10. Galium boreale. Northern bedstraw.
11. Helenium autumnale. Sneezeweed.
12. Helianthus giganteus. Giant sunflower.
13. Helianthus lætiflorus. Showy sunflower.

14. Helianthus mollis. Hairy sunflower. Circular 170, Fig. 62.
15. Heliopsis lævis. Pitcher's ox-eye.
16. Phlox divaricata. Wild blue phlox. See Fig. 72 and Circular 170, Fig. 69. *Rudbeckia purpurea.* See Echinacea.
17. Rudbeckia speciosa (*R. Newmanni*). Showy coneflower.
18. Rudbeckia subtomentosa. Sweet coneflower. Similar to Fig. 69.
19. Rudbeckia triloba. Thin-leaved coneflower. (Biennial, but self-sows.) Similar to Circular 170, Figs. 81, 82.
20. Sedum ternatum. Wild stonecrop.
21. Solidago Riddelli. Riddell's goldenrod. (Collect.)
21a. Solidago Virgaurea, var. nana. Dwarf goldenrod.
b. For shady places.
22. Adiantum pedatum.* Maidenhair fern.
23. Aralia racemosa.* Wild spikenard.

GROUP 2. SHRUBS.
42. Cornus stolonifera. Red-osier dogwood.
43. Sambucus canadensis. American black elder. Inside front cover and Figs. 4, 5, 65.
44. Sambucus canadensis, var. acutiloba. Illinois cut-leaved elder. Figs. 2, 46.
45. Sambucus pubens (*S. racemosa* of some nurseries). American red elder.
46. Viburnum cassinoides. Appalachian tea.
47. Viburnum dentatum. Arrow-wood.
48. Viburnum molle. Soft-leaved viburnum.
49. Viburnum Opulus. High-bush cranberry. (The native form, known as *V.*

24. Thalictrum polygamum* (*T. Cornuti*). Fall meadow rue.
25. Thalictrum dioicum.* Early meadow rue.
c. For water gardens or wet soil.
26. Asclepias incarnata. Swamp milkweed.
27. Eupatorium perfoliatum. Boneset.
28. Eupatorium purpureum. Joe-Pye weed.
29. Eupatorium urticæfolium (*E. ageratoides*). White snakeroot.
30. Nelumbo lutea (*Nelumbium luteum*). American lotus.
31. Nymphaea odorata. Sweet-scented water lily. Figs. 2, 48.
d. For very dry soil, for example, roadsides.
32. Monarda fistulosa. Wild bergamot.
33. Silphium integrifolium. Entire-leaved rosin-weed.
34. Silphium lacinatum. Compass plant. (Often native to moist meadows.)

americanum, is said to be freer from plant lice than the European). Circular 170, Figs. 77, 78.
c. Tall shrubs, ordinarily 7 to 10 ft. in cult.
50. Aralia spinosa.* Hercules' club.
51. Cornus alternifolia.* Alternate-leaved dogwood.
52. Cornus rugosa (*C. circinata*).* Round-leaved dogwood.
53. Hamamelis virginiana.* Witch hazel.
54. Physocarpus opulifolius (*Spiraea opulifolia. Opulaster opulifolia*). Ninebark.
55. Viburnum Lentago. Sheepberry. Circular 170, Figs. 55, 56.
56. Viburnum prunifolium. Black haw.

a. Low shrubs, ordinarily 4 ft. or less in cult.
35. Ceanothus americanus. New Jersey tea.
36. Ceanothus ovatus. Illinois redroot.
37. Hydrangea arborescens. Wild hydrangea.
38. Viburnum acerifolium. Maple-leaved arrow-wood. Circular 170, Figs. 39, 40.
39. Viburnum pubescens. Downy-leaved arrow-wood. See Fig. 40 and Circular 170, Figs. 37, 38.
b. Medium-high shrubs, ordinarily 5 to 6 ft.
40. Cornus Amomum (*C. sericea*). Silky dogwood. Circular 170, Figs. 79, 80.
41. Cornus racemosa (*C. paniculata*).* Gray dogwood. Branches stratified on old plants.

57. Aesculus glabra.* Ohio or fetid buckeye.
58. Amelanchier canadensis* (*A. Botryapium*). June-berry. (Stratified when old.) See Fig. 78.
59. Amelanchier lævis (*A. canadensis* of some nurserymen).* Smooth june-berry.
60. Carpinus caroliniana.* American hornbeam. Blue beech. Fig. 70.

GROUP 3. SMALL TREES.
61. Cornus florida.* Flowering dogwood. Not hardy north. Circular 170, Fig. 110.
62. Crataegus Crus-galli.* Cockspur thorn.
63. Crataegus mollis. Red-fruited thorn. Red haw. Fig. 71.
64. Crataegus Phaenopyrum (*C. cordata*). Washington thorn.
65. Crataegus punctata.* Dotted haw.

66. Crataegus tomentosa.* Pear thorn. (Branches sometimes stratified.) *Hawthorns.* See Figs. 1, 3, 7, 12, 62, 64, 66, 71, 79, 91.
67. Pyrus ioensis* (*Malus ioensis*). Prairie or western crab apple. Fig. 52. Sometimes cataloged as P. coronaria.
68. Sorbus americana (*Pyrus americana*). American mountain ash.

GROUP 4. TALL AND MEDIUM-HIGH TREES.

69. Acer rubrum.* (Thrives in some parts of Illinois, but rarely colors highly, and needs moist soil.)
70. Acer saccharum.* Sugar maple.
71. Aesculus octandra.* Sweet buckeye.
72. Fagus grandifolia (*F. americana*).* American beech. Generally fails on prairie and near Chicago, but thrives in some parts of Illinois.)

73. Fraxinus americana (*F. alba*).* White ash.
74. Fraxinus lanceolata.* Green ash.
75. Fraxinus quadrangulata.* Blue ash.
76. Gleditsia triacanthos.* Honey locust.
77. Liquidambar styraciflua.* Sweet gum.
78. Nyssa sylvatica.* Tupelo, pepperidge, or black gum. Fig. 68.

GROUP 5. EVERGREENS.
87. Pinus Strobus.* White pine. (Needs drainage.) See Figs. 77, 87.

79. Quercus alba.* White oak. Circular 170, Figs. 23, 58, 60.
80. Quercus coccinea.* Scarlet oak.
81. Quercus imbricaria.* Shingle oak.
82. Quercus palustris.* Pin oak.
83. Quercus bicolor (*Q. platanoides*).* Swamp white oak. See Fig. 67.
84. Quercus rubra.* Red oak.
85. Sassafras officinale.* Sassafras.

86. Juniperus communis, var. depressa (*J. canadensis*).* Canadian juniper.

Class II.   Non-Stratified Materials that are Reminders of Illinois

(For their practical uses see page 23. Incidentally they may remind one of Illinois, because they are native to the state.)

GROUP 1. PERENNIALS AND NEAR-PERENNIALS.

a. For garden cultivation in full sun.

88. Anemone canadensis (*A. pennsylvanica*). Round-leaved anemone.
89. Baptisia australis. Blue wild indigo.
90. Baptisia tinctoria. Yellow indigo.
91. Camassia esculenta (*C. Fraseri*). Prairie hyacinth.
92. Cassia marylandica. American senna.
93. Dodecatheon Meadia. Shooting star.
94. Erysimum asperum, var. arkansanum (*E. arkansanum*). Prairie wallflower.
95. Hibiscus Moscheutos. Swamp rose mallow. Circular 170, Fig. 105.
96. Liatris pycnostachya. Prairie button.
97. Liatris scariosa. Large button snakeroot.
98. Lilium philadelphicum. Wild red lily, (Bulb.)
99. Lobelia cardinalis. Cardinal flower.
100. Pentstemon laevigatus, var. Digitalis (*P. Digitalis*). Foxglove beard-tongue.

101. Phlox maculata. Early phlox. (Miss Lingard the favorite variety.)
102. Phlox paniculata. Garden or perennial phlox.
103. Physostegia virginiana. Obedient plant.
104. Sanguinaria canadensis. Bloodroot.
105. Tradescantia virginiana. Spiderwort.
106. Ulmaria rubra (*Spiraea lobata, S. palmata*). Queen-of-the-prairie.

b. For shady places.

107. Aquilegia canadensis. Wild columbine.
108. Asarum canadense. Wild ginger.
109. Campanula rotundifolia. Harebell.
110. Cimicifuga racemosa. Black snakeroot.
111. Collinsia verna. Blue-eyed Mary. (Biennial but self-sows.)
112. Erythronium albidum. White adder's tongue. (Bulb.)
113. Hepatica triloba. Hepatica.
114. Lilium canadense. Wild yellow lily. (Bulb.)
115. Lilium superbum. American turk's cap lily. (Bulb.)

116. Mertensia pulmonarioides (*M. virginica*). American bluebell. Fig. 38. Circular 170, Fig. 67.
117. Silene virginica. Fire pink.
118. Trillium grandiflorum. Large-flowered trillium.

c. For water gardens or moist places.

119. Acorus Calamus. Sweet flag. (Collect.) Fig. 36.
120. Arisaema triphyllum. Jack-in-the-pulpit.
121. Calamagrostis canadensis. Blue-joint. (Collect.) Fig. 48.
122. Caltha palustris. Marsh marigold.
123. Iris versicolor. Larger blue-flag.
124. Lobelia cardinalis. Cardinal flower.
125. Sagittaria latifolia (*S. variabilis*). Arrowhead. (Collect.) Fig. 46.
126. Sparganium eurycarpum. Broad-fruited bur reed. (Collect.)
127. Typha angustifolia. Narrow-leaved cattail. (Collect.) Fig. 2.

GROUP 2. SHRUBS.

a. Low shrubs, ordinarily 4 ft. or less in cult.

128. Amelanchier alnifolia. Northwestern june-berry. Dwarf june-berry.
129. Amelanchier alnifolia, var. pumila.
130. Diervilla Lonicera (*D. trifida*). Northern bush honeysuckle.
131. Evonymus obovatus. Running strawberry bush. See 163.
132. Prunus pumila. Sand cherry.
133. Rhus canadensis (*R. aromatica*). Fragrant sumac.
134. Ribes americanum (*R. floridum*). American black currant.
135. Rosa virginiana (*R. blanda*). Smooth rose.
136. Rosa carolina. Swamp rose.
137. Rosa humilis. Low rose.
138. Rosa lucida. Glossy rose.
139. Rosa setigera. Illinois or prairie rose.

Figs. 14, 39. Circular 170, Figs. 44, 76, 83.

140. Rubus hispidus. Running swamp blackberry.
141. Symphoricarpos occidentalis. Wolfberry.
142. Symphoricarpos vulgaris. Indian currant.

b. Medium-high shrubs, ordinarily 5 to 6 ft. in cultivation.

143. Corylus americana. American hazel.
144. Evonymus americana (*Evonymus*). Strawberry bush.
145. Ilex verticillata. Winterberry.
146. Rhus copallina. Black sumac.
147. Rhus glabra. Common sumac.
148. Ribes aureum (*R. odoratum*). Flowering currant.
149. Ribes Cynosbati. Wild gooseberry.
149½. Salix interior (*S. longifolia*). Sunset willow. (Collect.)

150. Spiraea alba (*S. lanceolata*). Western meadow-sweet.
151. Symphoricarpos racemosus. Snowberry.
152. Xanthoxylum americanum. Prickly ash. See No. 159.

c. Tall shrubs, ordinarily 7 to 10 ft. in cult.

153. Aronia arbutifolia (*Pyrus arbutifolia, Sorbus arbutifolia*). Red chokeberry.
154. Aronia melanocarpa (*Pyrus nigra, Sorbus melanocarpa*). Black chokeberry.
155. Benzoin aestivale (*B. odoriferum, Lindera Benzoin*). Spicebush.
156. Cephalanthus occidentalis. Buttonbush.
157. Rhus typhina (*R. hirta*). Staghorn sumac. Fig. 22.
158. Staphylea trifolia. American bladdernut.
159. Xanthoxylum americanum (*Zanthoxylum*). Prickly ash. For screens and barriers. See No. 152.

GROUP 3. VINES.

160. Ampelopsis cordata (*Vitis indivisa*). Simple-leaved ampelopsis. *Ampelopsis Engelmanni* and *quinquefolia*. See Parthenocissus.
161. Celastrus scandens. Bittersweet. Circular 170, Fig. 47.
162. Clematis virginiana. Wild clematis.
163. Evonymus obovatus. Running strawberry bush. See No. 131. Grape, wild. Figs. 74, 75.
164. Lonicera sempervirens. Trumpet honeysuckle. (Southern and central Illinois.)

165. Lonicera Sullivantii. Minnesota honeysuckle.
166. Parthenocissus quinquefolia (*Ampelopsis quinquefolia*). Circular 170, Fig. 45.
167. Parthenocissus quinquefolia, var. Engelmanni (*Ampelopsis Engelmanni*). Illinois creeper or Engelmann's ivy.
168. Rosa setigera. Illinois or prairie rose.

See Fig. 39 and Circular 170, Figs. 14, 42, 43, 71.

169. Rubus hispidus. Running swamp blackberry.
170. Tecoma radicans. Trumpet creeper. Circular 170, Fig. 66.
171. Vitis aestivalis. Summer grape.
172. Vitis bicolor. Northern fox grape.
173. Vitis cinerea. Sweet winter grape.
174. Vitis cordifolia. Winter or frost grape.
175. Vitis vulpina (*V. riparia*). Riverbank grape.

GROUP 4. SMALL TREES.

176. Cercis canadensis. Redbud.
177. Prunus americana. Wild plum.

178. Ptelea trifoliata. Wafer ash. Hop tree.

179. Pyrus coronaria. Narrow-leaved or eastern crab apple.

GROUP 5. TALL AND MEDIUM-HIGH TREES.

180. Betula papyrifera. Canoe birch.
181. Catalpa speciosa. Western catalpa.
182. Celtis occidentalis. Hackberry. Fig. 24.
183. Gymnocladus dioica (*G. canadensis*). Kentucky coffee tree.
184. Juglans nigra. Walnut. Fig. 17.
185. Liriodendron Tulipifera. Tulip tree. Circular 170, Fig. 110.
186. Magnolia acuminata. Cucumber tree.

187. Morus rubra. Red mulberry.
188. Platanus occidentalis. Buttonball. Sycamore.
189. Populus grandidentata. Gray poplar.
190. Populus deltoides. Cottonwood.
191. Prunus serotina. Wild black cherry.
192. Prunus pennsylvanica. (*Cerasus pennsylvanica*). Wild red cherry.

193. Quercus macrocarpa. Bur or mossy-cup oak.
193½. Salix vitellina. Yellow willow.
194. Taxodium distichum. Bald cypress.
195. Tilia americana. American linden or basswood. Fig. 3.
196. Tilia heterophylla. White basswood.
197. Ulmus americana. American elm. Fig. 3. Circular 170, Fig. 59.

GROUP 6. EVERGREENS.

198. Juniperus virginiana. Red cedar. Fig. 47. Circular 170, Figs. 9, 30.

199. Thuya occidentalis. American arborvitae. Circular 170, Fig. 10.

X—Some Uses for Illinois Materials

I. THE COMMON PROBLEMS OF SMALL HOME GROUNDS

1. Foundation Planting

THE nearer the house the more exacting are the conditions and the more conventional must be the planting materials. A higher percentage of foreign and horticultural varieties is permissible here than anywhere, save in the garden. Unfortunately, the favorites are grossly overplanted, especially the "inevitable three"—Japanese barberry, Van Houtte's spirea, and Hydrangea paniculata, var. grandiflora, all of which are foreign. Their brilliancy soon becomes commonplace, or tiresome, especially when a house is surrounded by barberry or spirea alone. It is better to have variety enough to furnish some flowers or color for every month. Try to have half the materials or more native to Illinois. In arranging the materials leave one or more attractive parts of the foundation unplanted. Put the tallest shrubs at the corners, angles, and against high foundations. In front of windows a carpet of trailing juniper may be suitable. The plants marked † are often called "coarse" by some landscape gardeners, who consider them unsuitable for the most refined surroundings. Others declare that ordinary foundation planting is pitifully weak, thru over-refinement, and that large buildings require large shrubs with large leaves for proper proportion. They prefer more virility and therefore believe in using hawthorns and even sumacs against some foundations, especially farmhouses and tall buildings. If more flowers are desired than bushes furnish, the shrubbery can be edged or carpeted in places with trailing myrtle and daffodils or Darwin tulips.

FOR THE SUNNY SIDE OF THE HOUSE

Low Shrubs.—(About 3 to 4 feet high.) Native: Rosa setigera, Rosa nitida, Rhus aromatica, Rosa lucida,‡ Diervilla Lonicera‡ and sessilifolia,‡ Hydrangea arborescens and var. grandiflora. Foreign: Berberis Thunbergii, Spiraea japonica, var. alba, Taxus cuspidata and var. brevifolia.

Medium shrubs.—(About 5 to 6 feet high.) Native: Viburnum dentatum, Rhus copallina. Foreign: Berberis vulgaris, Forsythia intermedia, Ligustrum Ibota, var. Regelianum, Lonicera Morrowi, Rosa rugosa, Spiraea arguta, Magnolia stellata.

High shrubs.—(About 8 to 10 feet high.) Native: Viburnum prunifolium, Lentago, and Opulus.‡ Foreign: Forsythia intermedia, var. Fortunei, Lonicera tatarica, Philadelphus coronarius, Syringa vulgaris,‡ Viburnum tomentosum, Viburnum Lantana.

FOR THE SHADY SIDE OF THE HOUSE

Low shrubs—(About 3 to 4 feet high.) Native: Rhus aromatica, Hydrangea arborescens, Symphoricarpus vulgaris, Ceanothus americanus, Taxus canadensis. Foreign: Spiraea japonica, var. alba.

Medium shrubs.—(About 5 to 6 feet high.) Native: Cornus racemosa, Viburnum cassinoides, Symphoricarpus racemosus, Ribes aureum.‡ Foreign: Aralia pentaphylla, Forsythia intermedia, Ligustrum Ibota, var. Regelianum.

High shrubs.—(About 8 to 10 feet high.) Native: Viburnum Opulus,‡ Physocarpus opulifolia.‡ Foreign: Forsythia intermedia, var. Fortunei, Ligustrum Ibota, Ligustrum amurense, Cornus alba, var. sibirica.‡

2. Vines for Porches and House Walls

For full lists of native vines, see page 25, Nos. 160-175.

On brick, stone, or rough concrete, use the self-supporting kinds, like Ampelopsis Engelmanni, which is hardier than A. Veitchii.

On a wooden house avoid the above and use a trellis or strong wire fastened with hooks so that vines can be laid down when the house is painted. Ampelopsis quinquefolia, Celastrus scandens, Clematis virginiana, Rosa setigera.

For front porch or refined surroundings, Akebia quinata, Clematis paniculata, Rambler and Memorial rose hybrids (not very hardy in northern Illinois), Rosa setigera, Wistaria chinensis.

On back porch. The following may be too coarse for the front of a fine house. Celastrus scandens,‡ Tecoma radicans,‡ wild grapes,‡ and Lonicera japonica, var. Halliana.‡

On the shady side. Ampelopsis Engelmanni and quinquefolia, Lonicera Halliana, Vitis Labrusca, Vinca minor.

3. To Frame the View of the House

For small houses, hawthorns and Cornus florida. For large houses, Ulmus americana, Quercus rubra, Acer saccharum, Tilia americana.

4. Borders

(Numbers refer to species on pages 24, 25.) Perennials for sunny borders: 1-21, 88-106. Perennials for shade: 22-25, 107-118. Low shrubs: 35-39, 128-142. Medium shrubs: 40-49, 143-159. Tall shrubs: 50-56, 153-159. Small trees: 57-68, 176-179.

Arbors and Pergolas

Hawthorns (62-66) make natural arbors of great beauty in Illinois. Climbers for arbors and pergolas 160-162, 164, 166-168, 170-175.

Banks

Shrubs and creepers are cheaper to maintain than grass, for banks are hard to mow. To hide useless terraces and bad grading, arching shrubs like 139 and 142, and rampant vines like 166 and 168, and 170-175, are useful.

Bird Gardens

Elders attract and feed with their berries sixty-seven species of birds; shrubby dogwoods, forty-seven; sumacs, forty-four; juneberries, twenty; and hawthorns, twelve. Other important groups are Juniperus, Ribes, Rosa, Viburnum, and Vitis. See Farmers' Bulletin 621, U. S. Department of Agriculture.

Bluffs

For permanent effect 87, 195, 196, 198. For immediate effect, plant thickly cheap native stock in variety, especially suckering plants like locust, 42, 43, 142, 148, 157, 159, and rampant vines like 161-162, 166, 171-175. Plants that lean over the top of bluffs are 57-61, and 176, while 149 and 166 hang far down.

Clay Soils (Heavy)

Trees: 70, 84. Shrubs: 46-49, 135, 137-139.

Color

Middle-western perennials are classified by color and season of bloom in Bailey's "Standard Cyclopedia of Horticulture," vol. 3, pp. 1469, 1470.

Cut Flowers

Perennials: 4, 9-20, 96-97, 101-102. For lightening bouquets of sweet peas, 10 is a good

II. SPECIAL PROBLEMS

(Numbers refer to species on pages 24, 25.)

substitute for Gypsophila paniculata, which fails in Illinois, according to Augustine.

Dry Soil

The following are great drought-resisters, most of them growing wild in sandy soil. Perennials: 2, 8, 20, 21, 32-34, 89. Shrubs: 35, 132, 133, 137, 143, 146-147, 157. Vines: 161, 166, 174. Trees: 58, 76, 79, 84-85, 178, 180. Evergreens: 86, 198.

Edging

Flower beds: 104. Shrubbery beds: 133, 142.

Meadows

Bulbs for naturalizing in meadows: 91, 93, 98, 114-115.

Poor Soil

See Dry Soil for many that will grow in sand. Juniper dislikes rich soil.

Screens

Rhus typhina. Morus rubra.

Shade

Perennials: 22-25, 107-118. Shrubs for shady side of house, see above under Foundation Planting. The following rarely thrive without shade: 38, 45, 52.

Street Trees

No species comes near perfection, but a satisfactory tree can generally be found in this short list: Red oak, American elm, Norway maple, oriental plane, sugar maple, pin oak, white ash, American linden, European small-leaved linden, horse chestnut. Avoid the short-lived box elder, soft maple, and poplars. "Green ash is better than white ash."—Burrill.

Trees for Northern Illinois

The following trees are characteristic of northern Illinois, but not of the central and southern parts, according to Burrill, and therefore should be planted freely in northern Illinois to intensify the natural beauty of that region: White pine, arborvitae, canoe birch, black ash, mountain ash, wild red cherry.

Trees for Central Illinois

The following trees are characteristic of central Illinois, but not of northern, according to Burrill, and may be planted to intensify the natural character of central Illinois: flowering dogwood, pin oak, shingle oak, sassafras.

Trees for Southern Illinois

The following trees are characteristic of southern Illinois, according to Burrill, and therefore, they may be planted to intensify the natural beauty of this section. American beech, sweet gum, bald cypress, western catalpa, silver-bell tree, basket oak, willow oak, cucumber tree, tulip tree.

Water Gardens and Water-Loving Plants

Perennials: 26-31, 119-127. Shrubs: 40-42, 136, 140, 145, 149½, 150. Vines: 169, 175. Trees: 69, 76-78, 193½, 194. Evergreens: 199.

Windbreaks

Instead of short-lived evergreens, like Norway spruce, Scotch pine, and Austrian pine, plant long-lived evergreens like white pine and hemlock. Instead of short-lived deciduous trees, like willows, soft maple, box elder, and poplars, plant long-lived trees like sugar maple, red oak, scarlet oak, or pin oak. "It may often be best to plant quick-growing trees, but if so, put them in separate rows so that they can be removed easily without destroying the more permanent trees."—Burrill.

XI—Literature of the Prairie Style of Landscape Gardening

THE following list makes no pretense of completeness. The subject is so new that the literature is fragmentary. The relation of each item to the prairie style or Illinois way is indicated. Where no name is given the author is the writer of this circular.

Agriculture

The Illinois System of Permanent Fertility. Cyril G. Hopkins. Circular 167, Illinois Agricultural Experiment Station. The Illinois system of permanent agriculture, when fully developed, will include permanent farm buildings and permanent planting materials, as well as permanent fertility of the soil. Often the orchards and the layout of the farm will be permanent. The Illinois way of planting is part of this larger scheme, since it uses permanent ornamental plants.

The Development of American Agriculture, what it is and what it means. Eugene Davenport in Report of the Illinois Farmers' Institute, 1909, pages 101-121. Contains on pages 108 and 109 a plea for the country beautiful, including a suitable country architecture and long-lived trees.

The Prairie Farmer's Creed. Clifford V. Gregory. Prairie Farmer Publishing Company, Chicago, 1912. Inspirational matter on a 9x12-inch poster.

Botany

An Illustrated Flora of the Northern United States. Britton and Brown. Scribner, 1913. Three volumes. Describes and illustrates all plants native to Illinois.

Catalog of the Flowering and Higher Flowerless Plants of Illinois. T. J. Burrill, in Ninth Report of the Board of Trustees of the Illinois Industrial University, 1878. The nearest approach to a Flora of Illinois. Though out of date, it is still helpful. A flora of the state is greatly needed.

The Flora of Cook County, Illinois. Higley and Raddin. Bulletin of the Chicago Academy of Sciences, 1891. Has been much used for restoration work in northern Illinois.

Flora Peoriana. Frederick Brendel. Valuable for restoration work in central Illinois.

Illinois As It Is. Frederick Gerhard, 1857. Chapter on climate, soil, plants, and animals by Frederick Brendel, pages 230 to 258. Describes plant societies of central Illinois.

Climate

Life Zones and Crop Zones. C. Hart Merriam, Bulletin 10, Division of Biological Survey, U. S. Department of Agriculture, 1898. Gives a scientific classification of American climates, including the three zones in Illinois, and names characteristic trees and crops of each zone.

Conservation

Report of the Illinois Park Commission for 1912, Springfield. Describes Starved Rock, White Pine Forest, and Cahokia Mound.

The White Pine Forest of Ogle County, Illinois. Free booklet published by the White Pine Forest Association, Mrs. J. C. Seyster, Secretary, Oregon, Illinois.

Ecology

The Plant Societies of Chicago and Vicinity. Henry C. Cowles. Bulletin 2, Geographic Society of Chicago, University of Chicago Press, 1901. Names the characteristic plants of fourteen environments, such as the ravine, river bluff, flood plain, prairie, etc.

The Prairies. B. Shimek in Bulletin of State University of Iowa, vol. 6, pages 169-240 (1911). Gives in tabular form over two hundred typical prairie plants of Iowa, and indicates the frequency with which they are found on flat and rolling prairie, ridges, openings, alluvial soil, and sand dunes. Explains treeless character by exposure to evaporation. Bibliography on origin of prairie.

General

How the Middle West Can Come Into Its Own. Country Life in America, September 15, 1912, pages 11-14. Mentions about fifty characteristic plants of the region from the Alleghenies to Omaha and from the Great Lakes to the Ohio river.

How to Heighten Western Color. Country Life in America, April, 1913, pages 80, 82, 84. Names twenty-seven species of permanent plants native to Illinois and the Middle West. Mentions twelve motives for unique gardens and cites western examples.

The Illinois Way of Beautifying the Farm. Wilhelm Miller. Circular 170, Illinois Agricultural Experiment Station, 1913. Names and illustrates many permanent planting materials native to Illinois, suitable for country and city planting. Has 112 illustrations.

The Illinois Way of Roadside Planting. Wilhelm Miller in Fourth Report of the Illinois Highway Commission, 1913, pages 334-345. Two illustrations.

The Illinois Way of Foundation Planting. Wilhelm Miller and F. A. Aust in Arbor and Bird Days, 1914. Department of Public Instruction, Springfield, Illinois, pages 7 to 19. Advocates foundation planting for school grounds and describes in tabular form twenty-six Illinois shrubs, giving season of flowers and berries, together with autumn or winter colors. Six illustrations.

Billerica. The North Shore Illinois Edition, issued monthly, beginning April, 1915, contains climatic charts, maps, and tables prepared under the direction of Warren H. Manning, Tremont building, Boston, and articles by W. C. Egan, E. O. Orpet, Emil Bollinger, Stephen F. Hamblin, and others. Concerns the region from Evanston to Waukegan.

Landscape Extension. Bailey's Standard Cyclopedia of Horticulture, vol. 4, 1915, pages 1813 to 1814. States aims, methods, and results in university extension work in landscape gardening, and cites several plans and plantings done by the Division of Landscape Extension, University of Illinois.

Illinois Examples of Landscape Gardening

An American Idea in Landscape Art. Country Life in America, vol. 4, 1903, pages 349-350. Describes and illustrates Graceland Cemetery, Chicago.

Reports of the West Chicago Park Commissioners, 1905 to 1908. Early illustrations of the Prairie River restoration and Rose Garden in Humboldt Park, and of the Conservatories in Garfield Park. Lists of materials planted and quantities used.

Landscape Gardening under Glass. Country Life in America, December 15, 1911, pages 10-11 and 50-51. Describes and illustrates Conservatories at Garfield Park, Chicago.

What Is the Matter With Our Water Gardens? Country Life in America, June 15, 1912, pages 23-26. Describes and illustrates the Rubens garden, Glencoe, Illinois, which is a spring, brook, and lake modeled on a prairie water system. This is also a restoration of vegetation native to the "North Shore" of Illinois.

A New Kind of Western Home. Country Life in America, April, 1913, pages 39-42. This article describes farm of F. O. Lowden, Oregon, Illinois, as type of country gentleman's estate in Middle West.

Bird Gardens in the City. Country Life in America. October, 1914, pages 58-59. Describes gardens of Albert H. Loeb and Julius Rosenwald in Chicago. The former is a restoration of plants native to Cook county.

Gartenkunst in Städtebau. Hugo Koch. Berlin, Wasmuth, 1914. Describes and illustrates work in Humboldt and Garfield Parks, Chicago.

Planting Materials

List of Perennials and Shrubs for Planting in Illinois. A. M. Augustine in Transactions Illinois Horticultural Society, 1913, vol. 47, pages 22-34. Gives in tabular form hardiness, method of propagation, value for cut flowers, etc.

Western Perennials for Western Gardens. Miller, Foglesong, and Aust, in Bailey's Standard Cyclopedia of Horticulture, 1915, vol. 3, pages 1469-1471.

Forest Planting in Illinois. R. S. Kellogg. Circular 81, Forest Service, U. S. Department of Agriculture, 1910. Describes the Urbana plantation and names, on page 30, the long-lived species for shelter belts.

Poetry

The Prairies. William Cullen Bryant.

The Plains. Lawrence Hope in "India's Love Lyrics." John Lane, 1908.

The Proud Farmer, The Illinois Village, and On the Building of Springfield. Nicholas Vachel Lindsay in "General William Booth," Kennerley, New York, 1913, pages 111-119.

Prairie Songs, especially The Call of the Wind, by Joseph Mills Hanson in Frontier Ballads. McClurg, 1910.

Scenery

Many contemporaneous descriptions of the wild prairie may be found with the aid of Buck's Travel and Description, 1765-1865, published by the Illinois State Historical Library. Springfield.

The Middle West—Heart of the Country. Hamlin Garland in Country Life in America, September 15, 1912, pages 19 to 24, 44, and 46. Popular account of the geologic origin of the Middle West and brief but comprehensive description of the following regions: Rolling prairie, Great Lakes, lake region, Dells, and coulees of Wisconsin and Mississippi river.

The Plains and Prairies. Emerson Hough in Country Life in America, October 1, 1912, pages 27 to 32, 50, 52, 54, and 56. Contrasts the humid and arid regions, describes some of the chief floral effects on the wild prairie, and declares that the landscape has had an important influence on human character.

Illinois Fifty Years ago. William Cullen Bryant, Prose Writings, Appleton, 1901, vol. 21, pages 13-22. Describes prairie near Jacksonville in 1832.

The Far West. Edmund Flagg, 1838. Reprinted in Thwaites' "Early Western Travels," vol. 26, pages 340-342.

The Homes of the New World, Fredrika Bremer, 1853, vol. 1, pages 601-603.

Illinois As It Is. Fred Gerhard, 1857. Chapter on "The Prairies."

Boy Life on the Prairie. Hamlin Garland. Macmillan, 1899. Describes Iowa scenes, but is largely applicable to Illinois.

The Prairie and the Sea. Wm. A. Quayle. Eaton and Mains, New York, 1905.

XII—The Showiest Plants in the World

GARDENESQUE MATERIALS ARE APPROPRIATE FOR GARDENS
BUT SHOULD BE USED SPARINGLY, IF AT ALL, ON LAWNS

MOST people are eager to avoid serious mistakes in landscape gardening, because no one likes to be accused of bad taste, and it is not pleasant to have one's home ridiculed. Singularly enough, most of the adverse criticism of home grounds comes from using the very plants that are generally considered to be most attractive in the world. People sometimes go so far as to impugn the motive of a lady whose home grounds are exceedingly brilliant. "She wants to appear richer than she is," they say. But is this fair and friendly? We doubt whether most people are really "guilty of insincerity," or "deliberately try to deceive," or "wish to make a vulgar display of wealth." On the contrary, we believe all their motives can generally be reduced to four innocent desires that may be grounded in instinct. For everybody loves flowers and color; everyone likes to have shade and beauty as quickly as possible; everybody likes a little variety or spice in life; and everyone has at least a rudimentary respect for neatness and order. Is it not possible that most of the alleged vulgarity is simply an excess of these virtues? At least the heart often tempts us to overdo a good thing. Suppose, then, we make the charitable assumption. Let us say that the motives are honorable, and the plants are attractive, and the whole question of good taste is simply one of self-restraint or of fitness. Figs. 82, 92. It may help us to understand why experienced gardeners sometimes abuse the very plants that seemed best to them as beginners, and it may be interesting to discover what plants these knowing ones now prefer. First, then, let us see how an innocent love of color leads beginners to buy the five classes of plants which commonly provoke the charge of bad taste or insincerity.

1. Bedding Plants

SUPPOSE you are an inexperienced home-maker—one of the thousands who are beginning family life every year in Illinois. You are afraid the place will not look well the first year. Even if you set out trees and shrubs it is obvious that the place lacks flowers. The florist tells you that tender plants will give more color than hardy ones. So you buy cannas, geraniums, begonias, or coleus, and in the kindness of your heart you put them in the middle of the front lawn so that every passer-by may enjoy them. How

cruel, then, for more experienced gardeners to say that you are trying to get the biggest show for the money! The kindlier thing is to explain to a beginner that tropical plants do not harmonize with a northern landscape, as hardy plants do (see Figs. 80, 81), and therefore it is more fitting to put tender plants in a garden and hardy plants on the lawn, for the garden or back yard is private, while the lawn or front yard is public. The showier the plants, the less we should expose them to every passer-by. It is a generous impulse that prompts us to share our greatest joys with everybody, but experience teaches that it is better to reserve them for family and friends than to force them on the public. It saves rebuffs. The quieter thing is in better taste.

2. Annual Flowers

A SECOND excess into which we are led by our innocent desire for color is to put too many annual flowers into the front yard. People who regard everything that is cheap and popular as "vulgar" sometimes speak slightingly of annuals, as if they represented a low degree of taste. Surely there is nothing inherently bad about the famous annual flowers, such as China asters, cornflowers, calliopsis, cosmos, pinks, pansies, poppies, stocks, and zinnias. On the contrary, refined people consider them quite appropriate to gardens. They are invaluable because they are the cheapest flowers of all and give results the first season. Every child should have a chance to grow the flowers that have charmed humanity for centuries, but the place to do it is in the flower garden, not in the front yard. Pure pink petunias may look very well when edging a garden path, but do they on a front walk? A straight line of scarlet sage may fit a garden, but does it look right when stretched across the front of a house? A bed of annuals may look very well at the edge of the lawn, but how about the middle?

3. Flowers of the Brightest Colors

A THIRD excess to which we are often impelled by this same innocent love of color, is the use of too many plants that have the strongest colors. One of the commonest complaints that ladies make is that "magenta flowers won't harmonize with anything in the house or outdoors, and we can't wear them." Gardening writers often express

the utmost animosity against magenta, as if it were a bad color in itself. Is any color inherently bad, or is it largely a question of combination? Most of the color discords in gardens are caused by the near-magenta colors, such as purple, crimson, and crimson-pink. So notorious are these "troublesome colors" that careful gardeners have a rule not to buy a phlox, peony, iris, or chrysanthemum from a catalog, even when they are advertised as being delicate colors like pink and lavender. Sad experience teaches that it is safer to select such varieties when they are in flower. If there is some plant of this color-group which you love very much, can you not harmonize it by surrounding it with a white-flowered variety, since white is the peace-making color among flowers? If not, it is easy to refine any near-magenta flowers simply by putting them in deep shade. But would the world come to an end if these "dangerous colors" were omitted altogether? What if a certain garden contained no cockscomb, Joseph's coat, spider flower, blue hydrangea, purple althea, Douglas spirea, Eva Rathke weigelia, Anthony Waterer spirea, or kochia? Would it be forever ugly, or are there enough other flowers in the world?

4. Showy Foliage Plants

A FOURTH excess to which many people are led by the desire for color is the use of too many plants that have extremely showy foliage, like the golden-leaved elder, golden mock orange, golden ninebark, and golden privet. Why do people who once grew these plants call them "yellow journalists?" Is there anything essentially criminal or low in them? On the contrary, they will produce more color at less expense than flowers, and at a distance they look like flowers. The first time we track down one of these gorgeous color masses and discover it is a showy-leaved variety of some familiar shrub, we are greatly interested. The next time there is a little disappointment to find that the wonderful new "flowers" are only leaves. After half a dozen experiences of the kind people begin to feel tricked, and some are so unkind as to call it a cheap way of making a big show of color. Flowers are finer products of nature than abnormally colored leaves. For example, coleus is probably the most efficient colorist the poor man can buy, and crotons are perhaps the most brilliant foliage plants that the wealthy put in their

80-81. Bedding Plants make the Biggest Show the First Year, but does Tropical Vegetation Harmonize with a Northern Landscape?
The bedding system gives more color than shrubbery during summer, but has no winter beauty, and the expense must be renewed every year. Fancy flower beds in the middle of a lawn make a home stand out in gaudy contrast to the surroundings; native trees and shrubs blend it with the landscape.

82-83. Good Taste in Landscape Gardening is largely a Matter of Fitness

These flowers are good, but are they not more appropriate in the back yard? One's taste cannot be questioned if the private part of the lot is screened.

In front yards, neighbors can cooperate to get long views, like the one at the right, by keeping them free from flower beds and by foundation planting.

lawns, but their flowers are inconspicuous or lacking, and so refined people say that coleus and crotons are like showily dressed people who are deficient in character.

So, too, with variegated plants, which have the leaves striped, barred, or spotted with white or yellow, like the famous little white-edged geranium we see in every park, which devotes itself so conscientiously to showy leaves that it hardly ever produces a flower. Why does the author of "The English Flower Garden" stigmatize them all as "variegated rubbish?" Because they are cheap? No, because rich people are much given to planting golden evergreens. Is it because variegation is often considered a sort of disease, since variegated plants are often less robust than their original forms? Not altogether.

The real objection is that plants with abnormally colored foliage often make a place too stimulating, the weight of authority being in favor of a restful place rather than an exciting one. Clear proof of this is furnished by places that are rich in magnificent specimens of copper beech, purple maple, and golden oak. Even the worst scolds among the critics concede that such plants are absolutely perfect of their kind. Yet the lawns of the newly rich are often overpowered by these superb trees—so much so that some unkind persons call them "purple cow places."

One of the most refined shrubs is the red-leaved rose (Rosa rubrifolia), a single bush

of which makes an exquisite accent, while twelve in a mass are merely showy. Almost as charming is a single purple-leaved barberry in the border, but what about a hedge of it across the front of the average city lot? And how would you like to have a nurseryman scatter over your lawn six or eight specimens of the purple-leaved plum which he calls Prunus Pissardi?

Probably the hardest plant for beginners to resist is the blue Colorado spruce, which is undoubtedly the showiest and most popular evergreen in the world. It is said that one eastern millionaire has planted $50,000 worth of it on his place. But in the communities that have had the longest experience with showy plants there is a quiet reaction against Colorado spruce, because so many places have been overdressed with it, just as some people have overloaded their persons with faultless jewelry. Around Boston, which is very rich in fine old examples of landscape gardening, the leaders declare that a single blue spruce is enough for a large estate and too much for the average city lot.

5. Everblooming Flowers

THE fifth excess into which we are betrayed by our natural love of color is the use of too many everblooming plants. Yet some of these often seem absolutely necessary for certain spots which ought to look neat and attractive all summer. That is why every formal garden is likely to contain a bed of

cannas, geraniums, or begonias. People who want a change from these sometimes use hardy plants that bloom two months or more, e. g., the Belladonna larkspur, Miss Lingard phlox, Napoleon III pink, Stokesia, Veronica subsessilis, or everblooming Lychnis. Those who like to have the prairie suggestion for a long time can get it from phlox, gaillardias, and mist flower (Eupatorium coelestinum). This is quite right, but should it be carried to the point of having more everblooming flowers than short-lived ones? If so, we have a show garden instead of a garden of sentiment. Which is better for the average family?

Have you ever seen a rich man's show garden dominated by everbloomers, such as cannas, geraniums, and begonias? It is certainly more gorgeous in summer than the ordinary hardy garden. And the longer the florists' creations bloom the more we admire their efficiency. But do they stir the imagination or touch the heart like the first glimpse of "daffodils that come before the swallow dares, and take the winds of March with beauty?"

"Fair daffodils, ye haste away too soon," mourns Herrick, and this is true of nearly every hardy flower, from spring crocus to autumn chrysanthemum. The very fact that they are short-lived is a part of their charm. The pang of parting with one favorite soon gives way to the pleasure of greeting the next friend in the procession. The garden of sentiment is dominated by hardy perennials like

84-85. Before and after Learning how to Arrange Showy Plants

"Like most people who move from a great city to a wooded suburb, I tried to save all the crooked, diseased, and short-lived trees. After losing four years I cut them down and filled the lawn with showy flower beds, trees, and shrubs."

"Finally I realized that an open, central lawn, flanked by masses of native trees, is better than a museum of costly curiosities. I now grow showy plants at the edge of the lawn only."—Wm. C. Egan, Highland Park, Illinois.

86. Mr. Farmer, why don't you Restore Illinois Trees to your Farmstead instead of Spoiling Illinois Scenery with Foreign Trees?

The settlers were excusable for planting the "cheapest evergreens" like Norway spruce, but can't you see how these spiry trees fail to harmonize with the characteristic beauty of middle-western woodlots and the dignity of your own pasture oaks? If you need evergreens, why not plant white pine? See Figs. 87, 88.

tulips, iris, peonies, phlox, pinks, foxgloves, Canterbury bells, sweet william, oriental poppies, larkspurs, and chrysanthemums. The flowers are all short-lived, but the succession is generally satisfactory. If not, perhaps it can be supplemented from the lists of perennials on pages 24, 25. The great thing for the millions is not the showy garden of temporary plants, which must be renewed every year. The great thing is the hardy garden of permanent plants. The fleeting flowers make less display than the everbloomers, but are they not in better taste?

If restraint be desirable in a private flower garden, how about the front yard? The beginner's ideal is to have a big show of flowers from spring to frost in both places. But is this either practical or desirable? If you go away for a summer vacation, what becomes of flowers in the front yard? Beginners commonly put an everblooming bed in front of the house, but it is generally more practical and in better taste to place it at the rear or side. The commonest mistake we make in America with everbloomers, especially near the front door, is to overdo the shrub that gives the most bloom for the money, viz., Hydrangea paniculata, var. grandiflora, a name which is contemptuously shortened by some to "p. g." But there is nothing to sneer at in a hydrangea, especially if it be put in a garden and allowed to assume its natural form of a small tree. Unfortunately, most beginners prefer to make a bigger show, and by following the florists' advice to prune heavily, they get a small bush that is covered with enormous, topheavy bunches of bloom. Look along an average American street next September and consider how much restraint has been used in planting the showiest shrub in cultivation. What about the walks, drives, and boundaries double-lined with hydrangea and nothing else? How about the front of a

house planted with hydrangea and nothing else? Can you not make the front door sufficiently attractive and more dignified by planting near it shrubs and vines that are presentable longer than flowers, such as the Illinois creeper or Engelmann's ivy and others recommended for foundation planting on page 26?

So, too, with the shrubbery border. There are comparatively few summer-blooming shrubs, but it is possible to keep up a show by using Hydrangea arborescens, var. grandiflora. The newly rich often try to beat nature in this way, but older families generally acquiesce in nature's suggestion that a place which is green in summer is more restful than one which strains to keep up a display of flowers. A famous example is the place which is often said to be the best example of landscape gardening in America, the Sargent home at Brookline, Massachusetts. It is natural for the beginner to think that flowers are more important than foliage, and to the heart they are. Consequently people often plant only golden bells, spirea, mock orange, lilac, and hydrangea, all of which are lovely in flower, but have little autumn color, and are devoid of color all winter. A week or two of bloom is about all you get from the ordinary shrub, and what you live with for six months is foliage. Consequently, landscape gardeners have a saying that "foliage is more important than flowers." The people are right in feeling that the average home place does not have color enough. Right here is where the expert planner does better than the beginner. He gives you more color thruout the year, but distributes it more evenly by using shrubs that have the triple attractions of flower, autumn color, and brightly colored berries or branches. Thus, on a well-planned place everyone's taste in color naturally becomes refined, and the eyes are opened to the quieter delights of form and texture in foliage.

Quick Growers

QUITE as laudable as the universal love of color is the universal desire for quick results, since speed has something to do with efficiency. Moreover, the quickest-growing plants generally cost the least, and are therefore doubly attractive to beginners. Unfortunately, the speediest plants are generally of short-lived efficiency or beauty. For example, the farmers must protect house and stock from the winter wind as soon as possible, so they commonly plant Norway spruce, Austrian pine, and Scotch pine, which generally lose their most valuable branches (the lower ones) before they are twenty years old, and turn a dingy brown or look unhappy. See Fig. 88. Granting that some of these temporary evergreens may be necessary, why not also plant some permanent evergreens, like white pine and hemlock?

With these evergreens the old-time farmer commonly planted box elder, soft maple, or willows to shelter house or cattle from the winter winds. The new-time farmer will avoid these temporary trees, if he can, and if not he will plant near them some long-lived trees such as sugar maple, and pin, red, or scarlet oaks.

City people want shady spots in their yards for rest and play, so they often plant soft maple or box elder or Carolina poplar, which are soft-wooded, like all quick growers, and therefore likely to be ruined by ice or wind storms soon after they attain a good size. Can they not get the shade they require in some other way, e. g., by means of a screened porch or summer house, or a large permanent tree?

Home-makers like to get rid of the bare look as soon as possible, so they often put a California privet hedge next to the sidewalk or at the sides of the lot, or they surround the house with privet. Unfortunately the California privet often dies to the ground in Illinois, and even where it is hardy it has little flowering, autumnal, or winter beauty. It is better to put the same money into three- to four-foot plants of Japanese barberry, Van Houtte's spirea, and golden bells, and set them against foundations.

Those who like to reap the rewards of foresight may congratulate themselves if they resist the allurements of quick-growers. And they will not have to wait twenty years to get satisfaction. Every day they see a town full of soft maple or box elder they will be glad they planted sugar maples or oaks.

Spectacular Forms

QUITE as natural as the love of color and speed is the craving for that variety which is the spice of life. Anyone who wishes to attract the attention of every passer-by to his place can easily do so by planting in his front yard one or more trees that stand up like flag poles. The most celebrated of these columnar trees is the Roman cypress, which is the spectacular feature of the famous old Italian gardens. The spectacular

87-88. Which Looks Better on Prairie, Long-Lived White Pine or—   Short-Lived Norway Spruce

Consider the value of these pines for windbreaks and winter beauty on this Iowa farm. There is enough roll here for drainage, which white pine demands.   Cheap, showy, and quick, but soon gets thin and brown.

tree of eastern formal gardens is the red cedar. The cheap substitute for these evergreens is the Lombardy poplar, which will shoot up faster, probably, than any other ornamental tree in the temperate zone. It will screen unsightly objects at the least cost and in double-quick time. It will grow on a city lot that is too small for an ordinary tree. Moreover, it often gives a pleasing note of uplift, which is a refreshing change in a monotonous environment. Even its short term of life can often be ignored, because the tree can be replaced cheaply and quickly. Any plant with such extraordinary virtues will always be a leading favorite, and, of course, it has been grossly overplanted. People naturally suppose that if one poplar makes a good accent, a dozen will look better, but is it so? One exclamation point may look well, but are not twelve in a row ridiculous? What about the ordinary city lot outlined with twelve to thirty Lombardy poplars? See Fig. 90. Too much accent is no accent, as the real estate dealer quickly discovers when he plants half a mile of street with nothing but Lombardy poplars. Overplanting of the Lombardy and Bolles' poplar is a city man's vice.

The corresponding vice of the country man is overplanting of Norway spruce. One of the leading landscape gardeners in the Middle West says, "The Illinois farmers often spoil the beauty of their farms by planting Norway spruce around their houses. See Figs. 86, 88. I call it the 'rip saw' because the ascending branches of this evergreen tear thru the sky-line of the deciduous trees in his grove or woodlot. I like evergreens and have planted thousands in Illinois, but the only one that harmonizes with the prairie is white pine, and that does not thrive everywhere. See Fig. 87. The crowning glory of the eastern scenery may be the army of evergreen spears that pierce the roof of the forest. Every landscape gardener who has come to Illinois has tried to reproduce that effect and failed, for Illinois cannot grow evergreens as well as the East. But this limitation is a blessing in disguise, for it gives us a chance to discover the peculiar beauty of western woodlands, which is the comparatively level sky-line and soft, billowy texture of our deciduous woods. This type of beauty is less spectacular, and may be poorer in species of trees, but it is exquisitely appropriate to so rich and peaceful a land as the prairie. To city people from the East it may be an acquired taste, but the farmers feel it. It is part of their faith that Illinois will become one of the most beautiful

regions in the world. And that is why I wish the farmers would chop down, as soon as they can spare them, the Norway spruces that murder our Illinois scenery."

"Another assassin is the Lombardy poplar (Fig. 90), which I call the 'butcher knife,' and I beg our wealthy people who plant it on their country estates to kill it without delay. It is impossible to find any plants that will make a more violent contrast with prairie scenery than the Norway spruce and Lombardy poplar. They are like the clash of drum and cymbals, for they demand instant attention from everybody. What they give to the prairie landscape is not accent, but shock. Accent is, or should be, intensification of the original note—not something surprisingly different. The accent-marks designed for the prairie by nature are horizontal haws and crabs, not spectacular poplars. (Figs. 90, 91.) It almost seems as if the great artist, Nature, purposely omitted plants with strong upright lines when putting the finishing touches on her most exquisite creation, the prairie. Even the red cedar, which is native to Illinois, hugs the lake shore or hides in wooded river bottoms; it will not thrive in the open, as it does in the East. My advice to clients is usually to kill Lombardy and Norway and plant prairie haws and crabs!"

Is it not barely possible that there are other ways of getting variety in home grounds than by planting Lombardy poplars? Two hundred kinds of permanent plants native to Illinois are mentioned on pages 24 and 25, about four times as many as a landscape gardener usually considers enough for the average city lot. Cannot those who want a change from the prairie get it by making their home grounds a snug harbor or retreat, instead of a museum? Why not surround farmstead or back yard with trees and shrubs, mostly native, and have a private outdoor living-room where one may entertain friends? Will not the prairie seem more beautiful to the city man by contrast with his home grounds? And will not home look twice as good to the farmer after a day outdoors?

89. Order is a Virtue, but Artificiality an Excess

Is not Catalpa Bungei overdone here and in many front yards, especially when double-lining walks and drives? Is it well to surround a house or lot with trees of one kind, set at equal distances in straight rows? (See Fig. 90.)

Weeping Trees and Shrubs

ONE degree less spectacular than sky-rocket trees are plants that seem to grow upside down, like the Camperdown elm or Teas' weeping mulberry. These are certainly legitimate in back yards, especially when trained for children's play houses, but are they usually appropriate in front yards? No doubt they attract more attention there, but they also provoke more ridicule.

There is nothing essentially ridiculous in a weeping willow, for a single specimen of the Babylonian or Napoleon beside the water may have considerable dignity, but a row of them has been compared to "hired mourners." Probably the most efficient of these professionals is the Kilmarnock weeping willow, which is the poor man's favorite, but equally absurd is the rich man's lawn if overdressed with costly specimens of weeping spruce, dogwood, and Japanese maples and cherries.

Such forms originated in the garden, as Manning says, and they belong there, not on the lawn. The weeping, cut-leaved, and spectacular plants are mostly horticultural varieties rather than natural species, and they are generally perpetuated by artificial means, such as grafting. They are one degree removed from nature, and to that extent may be considered artificial. For this reason, people prefer plants that are naturally pendulous, rather than artificially so. For example, they like the Wisconsin willow better than the Kilmarnock willow, which is so radically different from the normal willow. On the other hand, the cut-leaved weeping birch seems merely to intensify the peculiar grace of its prototype, the European birch. It is probably the most popular of all weeping plants and deservedly so, in spite of its rather short

90-91. Which is the Better kind of Accent for the Prairie, Vertical or Horizontal—Foreign Poplars or Native Haws?

A little accent is a good thing, but how about thirty Lombardy poplars surrounding a city lot? "All accent is no accent." Nature left the exclamation point out of Illinois scenery.

Some landscape gardeners will never plant the Lombardy poplar on the prairie. They say it makes too strong a contrast, while the haw and crab delicately accent the native beauty of the scenery. (A hawthorn in bloom.)

92-93. Good Taste in Landscape Gardening consists largely in Self-Restraint about the Showiest Plants in the World

"We made the usual mistake of planting too many rare, costly, foreign trees. When we learned better, two weeping trees equal to the above hid a view." "Finally we cut them out. (The ring in the grass shows one scar.) The finest specimens in the world are less important than good views."—Wm. C. Egan.

life. No wonder we see six trees of it in a city yard where one would be better, for it is easy to overplant the exquisite thing.

How many weeping plants can the average city lot contain with good effect? Some critics say "none at all." Others say "one— and that in the back yard."

Cut-Leaved Plants

LESS spectacular, perhaps, than columnar or weeping trees are cut-leaved plants. Certainly they are not so liable to criticism, and they are supposed to give refinement or elegance to a place. The standard of beauty in this group is the fern-leaved beech. Eastern people often are exceedingly proud of their fancy beeches, as if they had done a great deal to make them perfect specimens, whereas it is hard to fail with them. Unfortunately, beech rarely thrives in Illinois.

The excessive use of finely cut foliage often tends to make a place look effeminate, weak, over-refined. This is especially true of the front yard that contains half a dozen Wier's cut-leaved maple or cut-leaved birch.

The first time one meets a refined stranger on the lawn, it is pleasant to discover that he belongs to a respectable family, like the sycamores, lindens, alders, or hawthorns. But go to any big nursery and you will see that these supposed rarities are rather common, for most trees and shrubs of importance have their cut-leaved editions. Then comes a revulsion of feeling against reducing all nature's distinct leaf forms to a mass of shredded vegetable matter.

The reaction against "horticulturals" brings people back to nature with the question, "Is there not some simpler way of getting refinement in foliage?" Nature replies that she has adapted to Illinois the following trees with pinnate or feathery foliage: walnut, ash, Kentucky coffee, mountain ash, honey locust, and bald cypress. With shrubs of this sort she has not been so generous, but a variety of cut-leaved elder originating in Illinois is becoming a special favorite of our people. See Figs. 2 and 10. This plant is Sambucus canadensis, var. acutiloba.

Formal or Geometrical Plants

QUITE as natural as the love of color, speed, and variety is the love of order. A certain amount of formality is necessary, especially amid conventional surroundings. Unfortunately, this love of order runs to great excesses of artificiality, especially in the East, where rich men's gardens are often loaded with globes, cones, pyramids, cubes, and columns of evergreen foliage. The time-honored way of relieving flatness in formal gardens is to use bay trees in tubs. A cheap

substitute for these is California privet trained like a bay tree, and another is Catalpa Bungei, sometimes derisively called the "lollipop" or "all-day sucker." This has a legitimate use in formal gardens, but does it fit the front yards of Illinois? What about drives and walks planted with Catalpa Bungei and nothing else? See Fig. 89.

Double Flowers

A SUBTLER case of formalism which is overdone in many front yards in Illinois is the use of double flowers, such as flowering almond, flowering peach, Bechtel's crab, double lilacs, Paul's scarlet hawthorn, snowballs, altheas, and hydrangeas. Double flowers bloom longer than single ones and are, therefore, invaluable in formal gardens, especially in beds where a continual show of color must be maintained, but professionals generally agree that they are "too gardenesque for the lawn." Their single-flowered forms seem more appropriate to nature-like surroundings. Double flowers are artificial in the sense that their fullness is dependent upon man, for they go back to single forms if planted in the wild. Moreover, they generally tend toward one form—that of the ball—thus obliterating the individuality of the original flower. Consequently, many who retain the double flowers in the garden make it a point to have only single flowers on the lawn, e. g., single hydrangeas and single white altheas. Instead of the common and Japanese snowballs they plant the single-flowered originals of these, Viburnum Opulus and V. tomentosum.

In some cases, however, everybody acknowledges that the double flowers make a stronger human appeal, especially the "queen of flowers." It is the most natural thing in the world to put the common double roses in the front yard, but practical conditions are against that location. Garden roses have to be heavily fertilized and one does not like to have manure under the parlor window. The bushes must be pruned so severely that they are not presentable near the front door. Many beginners line their front walks with double roses, but is that the place to wage war on aphids, thrips, and rose-bugs? If we put double roses in the shrubbery, they will not hold their own against the bushes. Most people, after trying every location in the front, have taken their double roses to the back, but they preserve the rose sentiment in the front yard by planting the wild or single roses, of which a list is given on page 25 (Nos. 135-139).

The Evolution of Taste

IN short, the whole story of good taste in landscape gardening is chiefly one of fitness and self-restraint in the use of showy ma-

terials—plenty of them in the garden, but less on the lawn. It would be easy for us to betray the people's interests by encouraging beginners to plant anything they fancy in any way they like. But there is a chance to save the people of Illinois much money and time by pointing out the evolution of taste which communities and individuals commonly experience. To summarize it all, people generally pass in their appreciation from the temporary to the permanent, from the spectacular to the restful, from the showy to the quiet, from the artificial to the natural, from rare to common, from foreign to native. See Figs. 84, 85, 92, 93.

What can be done with costly specimens that are out of place? This is a painful question to those who have just learned that naturalistic surroundings are in better taste than the gardenesque. Three courses are possible: (1) remove them to the garden or back yard; (2) sell them or give them away; (3) use the axe. As an older editor once told an eager recruit, "The public may object to what you leave in, but they never miss what you cut out."

WE WILL

☐ Try not to overplant the things we love most, especially in the front yard.
☐ Plant our home grounds in the naturalistic style—not in the gardenesque.
☐ Move gardenesque materials from lawn to garden.

ACKNOWLEDGMENTS

Landscape Gardeners. The work of Jens Jensen is shown in Figs. 1, 2, 8, 10, 25 to 34, 36, 39, 42, 46, 48, 50, 56, 59, 69. The work of O. C. Simonds is shown in Figs. 3, 54, 60, 62, 67, 68, 71, 72, 94, 98. The work of W. H. Manning is shown in Fig. 44.

Architects. The house in Fig. 1 is by Louis H. Sullivan, who is generally considered the founder of the middle-western school of architects. Fig. 76 is by Frank Lloyd Wright, who first developed the type of domestic architecture which is called in these pages the "prairie style." (Mr. Wright declines to give or recognize any name for this work.) For the work of Robert C. Spencer, see front cover. Figs. 5 and 17 are by William Drummond. Fig. 11 is by Hewitt & Brown.

Photographers. The front cover, frontispiece, and Figs. 2, 3, 5, 6, 7, 10, 12, 17, 18, 24, 25 to 34, 36, 38, 39, 46, 52, 54, 57, 58, 60, 61, 62, 65, 67, 68, 69, 71, 72, 74, 75, 76, 88, 90, 94, 97 are by A. G. Eldredge. Figs. 9, 35, 41, 42, 45, 50, 53, 55, 56, 66, 86 are by or from Jens Jensen. Figs. 4, 13, 14, 73, 87, 89, 92 are by the J. Horace McFarland Co. Figs. 1, 8, 47, 48, 59 are by Henry Fuermann & Sons. Figs. 16, 82, 83, 95, 96 by B. A. Strauch. Figs. 15, 37 by H. J. Sconce. Figs. 19, 20 by L. D. Seass. Fig. 21 by L. E. Foglesong. Fig. 22 by C. N. Brown. Fig. 23 by A. G. Eldredge and F. A. Aust. Fig. 40 by Alfred Rehder. Figs. 43, 44 from Warren H. Manning. Fig. 49 from W. A. Simms. Figs. 63, 64 by O. B. Brand. Figs. 51, 70 by F. A. Aust. Fig. 77 by A. E. Ormes. Fig. 78 by Carl Krebs. Fig. 79 by Mrs. Lew Wallace. Figs. 84, 85, 93 from W. C. Egan. Fig. 91 by B. S. Pickett. Fig. 98 by Wasson.

Drawings on pages 4, 5 and "Done in Illinois" by L. D. Tilton.

The Illinois Citizen's Oath

Suggested by the Famous Athenian Oath Which Was Taken by Every Young Man When He Came of Age and Received the Suffrage

It has been proposed that graft can be largely prevented and the best citizenship promoted by a dramatic ceremony connected with the bestowal of political power. Every large park has some broad lawn suitable for public gatherings, such as ball games, folk dances, pageants, and political meetings. The youths and maidens, clad in flowing robes, may assemble in such a spot and make their vows of good citizenship according to the form in which each city chooses to express its ideals. At least one Illinois city is considering the best possible setting for great public gatherings where the city's aims may be expressed in dramatic ways upon occasion. Some of the sentiments expressed below have little to do with home gardening, but they have much to do with park design, which used to be the most important part of a landscape gardener's practice, and all must be considered in city planning, which is commonly regarded as the most important branch of landscape gardening today. The following is not recommended for any particular locality, but merely suggests some of the civic ideals that are commonly proposed by city clubs, chambers of commerce, and other bodies that usually attempt to express the aims of a community. Each town, of course, will wish to formulate its aims in its own way.

I will receive the right to vote as a sacred trust and always use it for the good of the whole community, instead of my own selfish interest.

I will vote for the liberty, health, and happiness of all my fellow citizens, not for the privilege of any class.

I will separate local issues from national ones and vote for the best man for each job, regardless of party politics.

I will assume all men to be honest and try to cooperate with public servants before criticizing them adversely.

I will strive unceasingly against graft, corruption, and inefficiency.

I will work for peace and try to prevent war—military, economic, and social.

I will practice moderation in speech and will urge toleration in matters of conscience.

I will help Illinois enlarge and improve her cities by promoting cooperation or emulation among neighboring communities, and I will not work against nearby towns.

I will help Illinois preserve and restore her sacred shrines of native beauty by extending the state and local park system for the recreation of soul and body.

I will do what I can to develop a living civic art, as the Athenians did.

I will endeavor to make my community so comfortable and beautiful that her children will always wish to live here and share in the perfecting of our civilization.

I will try to build a permanent home surrounded by many permanent plants native to Illinois.

As a public token of my loyalty I will plant beside the foundation of my home some Illinois roses to remind me and others of the "Illinois spirit."

I will work persistently to express the highest ideals of all citizens in a comprehensive city plan for extending, developing, and beautifying the city.

The Illinois Spirit in Landscape Gardening—Developing the Native Beauty instead of Copying a Foreign Type

Italy has her cypresses, Scotland has her pines, the East has her mountain laurel, and Illinois has her hawthorns, crab apples, bur oaks, and prairie rose. Does your community own a spot like this, which can be used for pageants, folk dances, readings, religious meetings, and the citizen's oath? (A scene in Graceland.)

Rogers & Hall Co., Printers, Chicago, Illinois

I Defy Anyone to Sell These Houses at a Profit

"This block of 'stickers' is the despair of every real-estate dealer. Not a tree or shrub. Telephone poles in the parking instead of in the back yards. You cannot expect to sell a bare property without serious loss."—F. M. Vanneman, real-estate dealer, Urbana.

All Houses on This Street are Readily Salable

"People are eager to live under these elms. I have sold these four properties a total of thirteen times. Each sale was at an increased price. It pays to plant permanent trees and shrubs according to a well-considered plan."—F. M. Vanneman, real-estate dealer, Urbana.

The Prairie Spirit

I BELIEVE that one of the greatest races of men in the world will be developed in the region of the prairies. I will help to prove that vast plains need not level down humanity to a dead monotony in appearance, conduct, and ideals.

I feel the uplifting influence of the rich, rolling prairie and will bring its spirit into my daily life. If my home surroundings are monotonous and ugly, I will make them varied and beautiful. I will emulate the independence and progressiveness of the pioneer.

I will do what I can to promote the prosperity, happiness, and beauty of all prairie states and communities.

I will try to open the eyes of those who can see no beauty in the common "brush" and wild flowers beside the country roads. If any souls have been deadened by sordid materialism I will stand with these people on the highest spot that overlooks a sea of rolling land, where they can drink in the spirit of the prairies.

I will fight to the last the greed that would destroy all native beauty. I will help my state establish and maintain a prairie park, which will restore for the delight of future generations some fragment of the wild prairie—the source of our wealth and civilization.

I will plant against the foundations of my house some bushes that will remind me of the prairie and be to my townsfolk a living symbol of the indomitable prairie spirit.

"Short Ballot" for Illinois Citizens

Let each family unite on some of the following propositions and record the resolution here as a reminder of the ideals they wish to accomplish during the coming year.

WE WILL

☐ Keep our home grounds clean, and screen unsightly objects by planting.
☐ Save old trees and plant long-lived species.
☐ Have an informal shrubbery border for year-round beauty instead of a trimmed hedge.

☐ Plant shrubs and vines against the foundations of our house. Plant permanent materials mostly native to Illinois. (See pages 24, 25.)
☐ Design and plant our home grounds or get the best advice we can.

HOW THE BALLOT-SIGNERS KEPT THEIR PROMISES

At the end of the second year the Division of Landscape Extension had 5,200 pledges "to do some permanent ornamental planting within a year." The signers were then asked to tell how they had kept their promises. Replies were received from 991, or 19 percent. of the signers. Of these, 785 spent a total of $75,117 on materials, plans, grading, lawn tools, etc. The average for the whole group of 991 was nearly $76. The average expenditure of 642 persons who spent less than $100 was $22. Let us hope that all readers of this circular will do as well or better.

What a Difference it makes in the Appearance of a Street if the Houses have Foundation Planting!

Shrubs are needed to remove the bareness and make a house look like a home. Sometimes neighbors cooperate and tie a whole street together by low shrubbery in the parking, as in the next picture.

Foundation planting gives a park-like appearance, especially when a block at a time is done. Around these foundations are many Illinois shrubs, especially roses. (Moeller and McClelland homes, Decatur.)